PAPERS IN ILLINOIS HISTORY

PAPERS

IN ILLINOIS HISTORY
AND TRANSACTIONS FOR THE YEAR 1938

THE ILLINOIS STATE HISTORICAL SOCIETY

SPRINGFIELD, ILLINOIS

1939

PRINTED BY AUTHORITY OF THE STATE OF ILLINOIS

 14

(80572)

CONTENTS

v

Official Proceedings, 1938:

ILLUSTRATIONS

FOREWORD

In presenting *Papers in Illinois History, 1938,* the Editor wishes to express his appreciation of the many letters of commendation which the first volume in this series brought forth. Within his knowledge no publication of the Illinois State Historical Society has aroused so much favorable comment. In many cases, the book's appeal led directly to new memberships, and was a not inconsiderable factor in the membership increase which has marked the year 1938-1939.

Most of the papers published in this volume were presented at the Society's annual meeting at Bloomington and Normal, May 13 and 14, 1938. The exceptions are "The Contribution of the Pioneer Printers to Illinois History" by Douglas C. McMurtrie, an address delivered at the Illinois Day Meeting in Springfield on December 3, 1937; and the articles, "An Illinois Martrydom" by Frank H. Dugan, and "Richard J. Oglesby: Forty-Niner," which are presented as contributions to Illinois history.

Occasional misunderstandings appear to make advisable the explicit statement of a policy usually taken for granted: While the staff of the Illinois State Historical Society takes every reasonable precaution to insure accuracy and objectivity, contributors, rather than the Society, must be held responsible for matters of fact and points of view.

PAUL M. ANGLE, *Editor*

MUST STATE HISTORY BE LIQUIDATED?*

By DIXON RYAN FOX

President James, and Fellow Addicts of History: I very much appreciate the generous and somewhat inflated characterization that the chairman has given me. I was particularly impressed by his reference to the occupational risks of my calling. We have on the Union College faculty a comic poet who recently set forth some verses on the college president, the modern college president, in which he rhymed the word with "non-resident." I am very glad to be here, although not simply because it is another opportunity to make a speech. I have found in my short four years of incumbency no embarrassing denial of opportunities of self-expression.

We inaugurated the twelfth president of Union College three years ago last autumn, and at that time we were very gratified to receive guests who came to pay their respects to the College. Among them was a distinguished Frenchman who had been sent by the Ministry of Education to inquire into the modes and processes of higher learning in America. He was particularly interested in the college president, for which there was no parrallel in the old lands across the sea. Hearing that one was to be publicly displayed in Schenectady, he came to see. Now the merchants of Schenectady very generously had displayed photographs of the new president, as a tribute and courtesy rather than as a work of art, in the windows along State Street. As this French representative came up he noticed them one after another,

* Dr. Dixon Ryan Fox, President of Union College and President of the New York State Historical Association, delivered this address at the annual dinner of the Illinois State Historical Society at Bloomington, May 13, 1938. The text is printed from a stenographic report.

and one in particular posted on the inside of the window of a restaurant. Just in front of the mouth of the photograph were these words: "Open Day and Night." We are now working on the night shift, and tomorrow I will be on the day shift.[1]

Of course this is a company in which one of my stripe feels very much at home. You are accustomed to education, and therefore you tolerate an educator. There has been a great deal of suspicion about educators in very recent times, from the little red schoolhouse up to the White House. They have been alleged to be impractical, happy-thought meddlers. I knew one of the most virulent sort, a psychological investigator who went around from school to school. He came into a classroom and said to those before him: "Now, children, I am going to ask you some questions, and from your answers I can tell what kind of minds you have." There was an embarrassed silence, and then he drew a long breath and said: "The United States is bounded on the north by the Dominion of Canada, on the east by the Atlantic Ocean, on the south by the Gulf of Mexico and the Republic of Mexico, and on the west by the Pacific Ocean; the Declaration of Independence was signed in 1776. How old am I?" There was no response at first, but after a little bewilderment one boy raised his hand and said, "Forty-four." "Indeed," said the psychologist, "that is extraordinary. I wish you would tell me exactly how you hit upon that perfect guess." "Well," said the boy, "I have an older brother at home, and my grandmother says that he is 'half-nuts,' and he is twenty-two."

Of course, I might seem to demonstrate the reasonableness of that deduction here tonight, but I think I am in friendly hands in an historical society. I have not been with you before, and therefore I am not in the danger, I suppose, I referred to when speaking to the American Historical Association at Philadelphia last December. I spoke there of another danger that college presidents are likely to encounter, that of being found out in

---

[1] On May 14, 1938, at a session of the Society held at the Illinois State Normal University, Dr. Fox spoke on the subject: "A Blueprint from American History."

repetition. I knew of one college president who went all over North America delivering his one address, which he gave under nineteen different titles; he went to the same city for three years in succession and made the same address. At the conclusion of his third performance he was waited on by a committee who gave him a very attractive velvet casket upon which he beamed with appreciation and received very graciously. He opened it and found that it contained an old-fashioned hunter-case watch; then he opened the case and found that it contained only a pencil note which read: "If you come back here a fourth time and give that same speech, we will give you the works."

But we are here to talk about history, state history and local history. On occasions such as this we seem to feel the living past, the past that urges or restrains our daily purpose, makes one course hard and another easy, as though unseen spirit fingers were intertwined with ours to lead us into paths that this historic past had made appropriate. We are, I think, aware of the use of history; we read it in order to understand ourselves. We read all sorts of history, but I think in this particular, local history is especially necessary.

In the pageant of the arts and sciences, I know that the local historian does not figure brightly. He is usually compared with him who writes of parliaments and armies, and since the whole is greater than the part, it seems impossible for him to be as great as one who chronicles the nations of the world. He is usually dismissed as an antiquarian, uncritical and queer, who painfully works out a record of the insignificant. Now and then there is a flash of sympathy for some Old Mortality chiseling afresh the memory of years gone by, but he is usually regarded as an eccentric, if not worse. And if there is one spectacle more forbidding to the general mind than one of these, it is a number of them gathered together as an historical society, because it is usually inferred that their interest springs from genealogy, and that genealogy springs from snobbishness. I think that is the popular opinion, and as popular opinion often is, is wrong.

We are concerned with the dead, that is true. But I think of the apothegm of Maeterlinck: "There are no dead." You will remember that this mystic wrote a play called "The Power of the Dead," in which is a scene where a host in a chateau is entertaining a company at dinner, guests who engage in ribald jests about portrait sculptures placed along the walls of the salon. The host becomes impatient and irritated, and finally says:

> They are jokes that should not be made when they deal with the dead, and especially such dead as these . . . . I have mine, you have your own; let us learn to show them due honour. . . . It is they that have made us what we are, and we exist only through them! . . . Not only are we what they were, we are nothing more, nothing else than what they continue to be! . . . Death has not carried them far away from us; he has planted them within us! . . . And now it is within us that they are, within us that they exist and have their being, and we are nothing but their shadows . . . . They are greater and more truly alive than we are! . . . When we forget them, it is our whole future that we lose sight of; and when we fail in respect to them it is our immortal soul that we are trampling under our own feet! . . . I pity those of you who do not grasp this truth; I turn toward those whom they have insulted; and with profound obeisance before their invisible presence I beg their pardon.

The past is in our blood; the dead live in our life. That is one of the strong springs of interest in genealogy, and makes it very reasonable for us to want to know more about ourselves, through studying, as it were, our component parts. There are incidents to that study that throw strong light upon history, the individual interest in American life, and the biographical illustration of the great historical movements. Genealogy, in itself, is justified by that higher self-consciousness and interest in our own composition.

But the dead are with us in our common life as well as in our individual life. We have, of course, their physical heritage. What a pity it would be, what a human tragedy, if we all had to be pioneers of every enterprise, if each generation took with it its improvements and its contribution! We know that we have inherited most of what we have. Those who have gone before built the roads that we improve, and use, and walk upon. They reared the buildings, some of which remain, and some of which have gone to make better buildings. They cleared the forests, measured the bounds of property, tilled the soil. I remember that last summer, while traveling in England, I saw many ancient stone bridges that were built in the eleventh and twelfth centuries. There they stand, not by reason of any contribution made by those who now live or who have lived for long since. Yet they are used every day, and I hope that somebody now and then uses them in gratitude.

The physical heritage is what makes possible for us a better world to live in, but it is by no means so important as the social heritage which comes to us from those who have gone before. It was they who set up our institutions, they who devised our social processes, for the most part. Indeed, by their experience they taught us how to live, so that we by getting more experience may teach better those who are coming. We are not the first nor the last of the human race; we are merely a link in a long and perhaps an endless chain. I think of ourselves not only as individuals, but as parts of the cosmic movement. It is, I think, not a depressing thought to feel that we are such in this sense—working out a great purpose or at least a great destiny which could not be realized otherwise.

But the main thing for us to remember as historians is that we are stewards of this past for the benefit of the future. We know that the present is a figment of the imagination; there is no present. There is a past, and there is a future, but the present is such an infinitesimally small point that it is always becoming the past. What seems to be the present is the result of the past. We hear complaint of the old *mortmain*, the dead hand that seems to throttle us, that lays upon us its impediment. But really the past sustains us much more than it restrains us or drags us down.

The social devices are many of them bodied forth in institutions. The local historian goes down the street of his village or his city, and he sees a church. He knows that that church was founded in 1820 or '30 or '40 because there were a certain number of people who believed in a certain way. They got their beliefs perhaps from Scotland, and the circumstances of Scotland in the sixteenth century become very pertinent to explain certain of the sentiments and interests of his town. The next church may extend back to Martin Luther, who seems to live in this village in Illinois by reason of what he did in the early part of the sixteenth century. Another church is in communion with that great world organization centering in Rome, and there is a background of centuries, now almost millenniums, that contributes to this faith. Those are historic origins which operate upon his village. And he goes on to another church, and realizes that this has had its origins in a national sentiment in England which challenged the ecclesiastical authority of that Roman church, and has bred a certain tradition, a tradition that functions in a seemliness of worship.

The historian, perhaps, should be accompanied by a little group of children. He sees the sign above a lodge door. When were lodges brought to this country? And why? How did they develop in response to some peculiarity in the American spirit, more healthfully, at least more generally, than in any other country? He goes by a mill. What was the type of industry that that mill represented? What did it succeed and what, in practical worth and value, has succeeded it? And how is it, then, that this community has profited or has been injured by the change from hand manufacturing to that which came from the harnessing of natural forces? He goes on to see a public library. Who was it that went from house to house to solicit funds to build that library? How was his faith kindled and how did he bring this important center of civilization to this town? He goes on to a post office. How was communication developed in this region? He passes a railroad station. What was it that made it possible and profitable to build this artery of transportation through this community? From the local examples this vision spreads not only to the whole history of the United States, but to the history of Christendom.

If there is any country which needs local history, it is the United States. We are still, as the traveler John Bristed said more than a century ago, the most locomotive people on the face of the earth. This has been due to the opportunity in the new and newer parts of this continent, so that we were always moving on to larger opportunities, full of faith, faith generally justified. There has been great importance in this living here today and there tomorrow, but there has been a loss of real home sentiment, such as is so potent a factor in the lives and dreams and contentment of men and women in the older countries of Europe. We very much need to cherish local sentiment, the idea of belonging to a place.

Much has been written in recent years of the sentiment of patriotism, something like nationalism. That is a very young idea in the history of the race; it hardly antedates the year 1500. Some have written to prove that it has been created artificially and steadily and skillfully promoted, but everybody recognizes as natural and fundamental the old loyalty, the passionate loyalty to a place or a region. There is a natural relationship of the individual to a place. And so I think we especially need to cultivate local sentiment. If the government is to place over us a director of our social policy, as it has directors of nearly everything else, it might compel us to consider local history. As good old Dr. Johnson said: "To abstract the mind from local emotion would be impossible, and it would be foolish if it were possible." It is such local traditions as we naturally cherish that enrich the associations of our hearthstone, and make life more interesting and lovely.

None of us are compelled to content ourselves with the neighbors that we personally know. There are a great number of other neighbors who are more or less distant from us in the field of time, but whom I have tried to show may affect our lives very much more than those who pass by our doorsteps.

The sentimental values of local history and state history are obvious to anyone who gives them but a moment's thought. There is also utility in local and state history. We need to know the community in which we try to bear our share and part; we need to know the influences that brood over it from yesterday in order that we may do our parts as citizens more usefully and more effectively. We know that what is appropriate in another place would not be in this, simply because of the manner in which this place came to be, and live, and grow. So from the political point of view there is much to say for local history and state history; they help us understand the communities in which we live and work.

And then there is the scientific value. It will not do to strain biological analogies too far, but in a sense the local historian is the microscopist of the body politic who looks down into a life where the individual counts, where the little groups of these cells come together as communities, and where one can watch persons in their daily life and work, and from this observation draw lessons of wide value exactly as does the scientist in his laboratory. Perhaps you have read Gilbert White's *Natural History of Selborne*. If so, you know that that book has long since been elevated to the level of a classic—a great piece of writing and of science. Another scholar who had the same degree of imagination, insight, and industry, could do as much for the human history of a community as the Reverend Gilbert White did for his small village of old Hampshire, England. Given the art, he could produce as authentic a masterpiece on the history of a county in Illinois, done as though he were writing the history of the world. The subject is not too limited for a great production. Only we need a genius to do it, if we are to lay it beside great masterpieces that have been done on a broader scale.

One of the great difficulties, I feel, with the work of state historical societies and of local historical societies has been a tendency at times and places to imagine that their membership is a special privilege of certain people—those who can trace their ancestors to the first settlers or to distinguished people. That, I am pretty sure, leads to dry rot. That, I am pretty sure, leads to and results in a society rattling around and atrophying in some stately old building that represents what once was a vital and a proud concern. That is what leads to dwindling devotees rehearsing old, old stories to dwindling audiences. History is a common influence; it is a common need; and therefore I believe that we have to welcome all those who wish to adopt our background. I feel very much at home in some foreign countries, and not so much at home in others. Last summer, for example, I spent some time in Turkey, and I felt anything but at home in Turkey. And then I lived for a time in Scotland, where I felt as much at home as when living in my own house. One can adopt the background of some foreign people if one wishes to and if it is congenial. But certainly if you go to live in a community, you should attempt to adopt the background of that community, and those who live there should welcome the newcomer with eager hospitality; they should be glad to share their background, and must share it if there is to be a community life that is healthy and pleasant for all concerned.

So local history becomes an enzyme that brings the community into health. Children of newcomers and their fathers and mothers feel more at home and are therefore more happy and more safe companions and contented neighbors if they can be persuaded to understand the background of the community of which they have become a part. Therefore I urge upon all societies to enlarge, and enlarge, so as to include as many people as can possibly be persuaded to cherish this local legend which means so much to the health of the community. I know of no way to make a stranger into a friend so effectively as to introduce him to your interests, particularly when your interest is in the home background of the place where he has come to live.

Local history has beyond this a value that has been hinted at but not very much explored tonight. I think it may be summed up in what Dr. Jameson once said: "Local history is national history locally exemplified." In it you find the microcosm of the whole of American history, and as I tried to show in speaking of churches, lodges, mills, and other institutions, a microcosm of all of the history of the western world. As it becomes illustrative, it becomes highly valuable as explaining how the human race, the whole human race has developed in community life.

There is, however, one danger which historians will do well to recognize and avoid—the danger of looking into the past only for those things which we think explain the present. That is frequently given as the chief argument for history, and perhaps it is, but it certainly is not the only argument. May I warn against the danger of present-mindedness, of thinking that the only things of value for us to know are those which seem to have led directly into our present scene. I spoke a few moments since of being in Turkey. I think I learned a good deal about America while in Turkey and in Greece, because these countries were so different from America. I came back realizing some of the features and characteristics of American life that I hadn't noticed before, because I had been to places where they were absent. For the first time I recognized some things that had played a part in my own life.

Just as travel helps one to appreciate his home—and by "appreciate" I mean to make a critical but fair estimate of it— so travel in time helps us to appreciate our present by throwing it against a background of a different kind. You know nothing until you know its limits; you cannot determine its limits until you see where it leaves off from being something else. Comparison is the soul of understanding. If I go back into Saxon England and read of practices and institutions so very different from those I know today, I begin to understand very much more clearly what I am living with today. So a history that seems to have no bearing upon the present may explain the present much more than precedents deliberately sought.

As to state history, Professor Frederick J. Turner had an interesting theory. He felt that we were giving too much time to its study. He said the states were many of them historical accidents—and that is particularly true in the West, where boundaries often were arbitrarily laid out in some office down in Washington. "They do not represent natural divisions of society." Perhaps they don't. He said, for example, that a river valley was a unit, and should be studied historically as such. Perhaps that is true. But it happens that you cannot study the history of a valley very conveniently because it had no corporate voice, it registered no opinion, as a valley. If you want to know what the people of that valley felt you have to go into the history of states that overlapped it and find how representatives from a certain county voted in this state, and how the representatives of an adjacent county in another state voted. If you find that they voted similarly, you may begin to understand the community of vision in that valley— but you get at it through state history. If you want to understand their church history, quite often you would have to go into the records of the state church society. After all, state history is essential since that is the form the record takes.

The American history that every schoolboy knows is not the most important part of the nation's past. With respect to the seventeenth and eighteenth centuries in America, too much attention has been paid by historians to the separate experience of the various colonies, without a generalized view. But once Washington had taken up command under the Cambridge Elm—if it was the Cambridge Elm—and certainly when he had taken the oath of office in New York City as President, then attention centered for a time on the Federal Government, a few months in New York, then ten years in Philadelphia, and ever since in the District of Columbia. And in the schools we have come to feel that the important things were foreign policy, debates about the tariff and about territorial administration, particularly with respect to the institution of slavery. Really those are not the important things that have happened in American life in general. Where do we go to find out about crime and punishment? About education? About arteries of transportation, roads, canals, and railway lines? Or the rules of acquiring and holding property?

Where do we find the guaranties to labor? Where do we find the registration of the public mandates with respect to lotteries and sport? These things which make up the most interesting part of the history of any country have been worked out here in the states.

Of course you say that this may be past. Perhaps it is. I hope it is not, because I don't think in a country of this size and population, with its variety of backgrounds and interests, that the thinking for every individual of every group can be done in a city of handsome buildings down upon the Potomac. I can think of a policy-determining officer stationed in the eighty-fifth floor of the Empire State Building, trying to regulate traffic on all of the corners he can see—perhaps the corners he cannot see. He can do a job of uniformity; he can perhaps see more economically, but he cannot see the personal problems of the man in the car as well as a policeman stationed on the corner. If he flashed his lights uniformly from the eighty-fifth story of the building and left nothing to local control he would have confusion right away. I think it will be necessary to have local government and state government, and perhaps a recession to the old style of politics to a greater degree than we have lately seen.

At any rate, when it comes to dignity of people, wealth and space, our states rank well with the nations of Europe. It would take three Denmarks to compare with the wealth and people of Pennsylvania; California outranks Norway about one-fourth with respect to people and space, to say nothing of its large margin in respect to wealth; there are more people in Ohio than there are in Australia; New York ranks with Canada; Texas is larger than Ireland in population, and you could pack seven Emerald Isles within its borders. Our states are not negligible; they have a dignity that comes from importance. It is true that their time span may seem to be short. Of course, that of the whole nation seems to be less than that of the nations abroad, but there has been more social chemistry at work in digesting many different kinds of people and institutions, more than could be found, I think, anywhere else in the world. So the history becomes as rich as that of a static community reaching down through many, many centuries. And, after all, the blood of Americans is as old as the blood of Europeans.

Great careers are not made down in Washington; no one nowadays is born great. Up to the end of the eighteenth century men were born great. In England if the House of Lords was powerful and one was the son of a peer, he was a great man ex officio. That day is past. Now careers become great by reason of local experience and local demonstration. I suppose you could write a social history of the United States—not a very good one, but some kind of a social history of the United States—out of the second chapters of American biographies. The first chapter usually states the genealogy; the second chapter deals with the local environment. It is that local environment that has made a man good enough to be sent to the legislature, to be the moderator of the church in his state, or whatever it may be, or makes him good enough in the state capital or in the state work to be sent into national service. The career, however, was molded and modeled in the state.

Certainly you cannot understand America from what goes on in the Federal Government. That is to say, nobody could understand Calhoun and his curiously interesting theory of concurrent majorities unless one knew of his experience in old South Carolina in 1810. Nobody could understand Theodore Roosevelt's attitude toward the courts in 1912 without knowing something of his experience as an Albany legislator in 1882. Nobody could understand the Free Soil Party who doesn't know the reasons for the breakup in the New York regency some years before. Nobody could understand either Mr. Douglas or Mr. Lincoln without knowing about their arguments in Illinois. Nobody could understand Douglas' movement in breaking up the Missouri Compromise who doesn't know something of the local history of Illinois and Missouri, and at the same time something of the railroads that were to serve them.

It is necessary, then, to know the background of these things, and the more so because nobody votes in Washington entirely on his own motion. Much is by instructions, more or less, from somebody back home. You cannot understand the *Congressional Record* without annotations from the local newspapers. We know full well that some of our foreign history, our foreign policy, and the history of our foreign relations have been produced by local circumstances—the Chinese Exclusion Act, for example. The Treaty of 1842 with Great Britain was based upon public sentiment in Maine and New York and elsewhere. The treatment of Mexico has been very much controlled by sentiment along the Texas-New Mexico-Arizona border. So it is necessary to have state history even to understand national history.

It is interesting to realize that in social history our sections differ, and words differ. "Temperance" in some places means or has meant "total abstinence;" in other localities "a light and moderate indulgence;" and in others simply "a condition of being less drunk." As to "woman's sphere," the term has had a different meaning, historically, in Wyoming from that in South Carolina. The observance of the Sabbath differs according to latitude and longitude in American history. Certainly the zeal for schools has differed as between communities here and there; the reverence for a family aristocracy which seemed natural by reason of tradition in one locality has seemed ridiculous in another.

Eli Thayer could take some New Englandism out to Kansas, to a new place, but what would have happened if he had tried to follow his original plan of making a New England Emigrant Society function in Virginia? We need to know the differences in local sentiment. This is not a country of one color; it is polka-dotted with many colors, and in order to understand it you must understand its localities and sections.

I want here to pay tribute to the historical societies which have cultivated this tradition; to their officers and presidents and secretaries and treasurers; to the committees that have with unfaltering faith and zeal sustained and increased the power of the historical forces; to the private—I was going to say the humble private in the ranks, but rather the proud private in the ranks—who has loyally paid his or her dues and supported a work that he or she feels is good for society, who knows that history is good for people and who wants to make it good for more people.

Historical societies, of course, need to cultivate scholarship. But they need very much, besides that, to cultivate a broader knowledge of history, or a knowledge more broadly held. That is propaganda; that is the word that scares so many of us. It has a very honorable past; certainly in the Catholic Church, propaganda has been a concept of the highest value. We may use a distinction between propaganda and "impropaganda;" we think that our side of things is all right, and that is propaganda, but what the other man is saying is wrong, and impropaganda. But I am all for propaganda when it comes to this exploring of the value of history, and historical societies have evangelically to promote this exploration.

You sustain museums. Now a museum is a very real responsibility; it means that you ought to have a good museum. That is an art and a science that requires a great deal of study. I would like some time to give a speech on museums, but I will spare you that now. That, however, is the way a great many historical societies are enlarging the number of people who are interested in history. Of course there are those who feel that a museum does not belong to the historical society or the historical society with the museum. That is not a practical question for those who live in small towns; for if there is to be an historical museum it usually has to be done by the historical society, which suggests a very large subject that I shall not try here to invade.

What I am trying to say is this: You have more than a hobby; you have a cause. That is the attitude which I think every member of an historical society—not only the officers—must take if the work is to be as effective as any other kind of work.

We can say that the work that has been done on local history in some sections of this country has been on a plane with the best of any other sort of history. I am here to say, ladies and gentlemen, that the State of Illinois has achieved a higher level of contribution in history than any other state in the Union. There are some reasons why that is natural. Illinois is in a sense a typical state; its varied interests are typical of American variety. It leads in agriculture; it is second in the value of its mineral products, and third in manufactures; and it contains the fourth city in the world. It has been a melting pot; if that metaphor characterizes America, it has boiled more furiously here than elsewhere. It is, of course, the crossroads, the railroad crossroads of the country. Its theme is a great one, but a great theme does not make a great six-volume history; yet the achievement of that history has of course held—not only gained, but held—the admiration of the historians of all this country.

In New York we recently published a ten-volume history of the state. It was an effort to imitate that of Illinois, but none of us who poured our energy and thought into it has ever for one minute thought that it compares with the *Centennial History of Illinois*. There is no other state that has done anything like it, and I am sure that no other state ever will. Now, what did produce this masterpiece? Well, it was produced because of two interacting causes, as always—leaders and followers. You have to have both, and in Illinois you had them.

I suppose the state was fortunate in that some of its early prominent citizens, particularly the governors John Reynolds and Thomas Ford, themselves wrote histories of the state. And then other prominent citizens, Sidney Breese, whom we are very proud to recognize as a graduate of Union College, and Ninian W. Edwards, and Elihu B. Washburne, wrote histories of the state. Among your journalists, Paul Selby and others have written distinguished contributions, and that undoubtedly has given prestige to historical writing. Nevertheless I think a great deal of it stemmed out of the vision and courage of one man—Clarence W. Alvord.

Mr. Alvord was a great man. He had a remarkable mind. I was going to say "a remarkably curious mind," and I am quite willing to admit the application in both senses. He had, of course, a mind that was strongly individualized, and therefore must have puzzled many people. But he had the courage and the grit and the tenacity to go forward with a great project. You will say I am telling you nothing that is new, but the new part of it is that I come from New York, and still I know it. I am voicing the opinion of the outside world, and we will see if it corresponds with yours.

Mr. Alvord in 1905 discovered the colonial records of Illinois. That was a romantic and a dramatic event. I don't know of anything as striking in American historiography as what he did in Belleville and Chester simply because he had a "hunch." He not only had this quality of leadership, but he had support. A manuscripts commission, as you know, was appointed to work upon these records. It was a great discovery in Illinois to find that you, just as Connecticut and South Carolina, and so forth, had colonial records. Then pretty soon the Historical Library began this remarkable series of extensive developments in source publication. Nobody else did anything like that. You had the bibliographies of two thousand pages that had been brought together by Doctors Scott, Buck and Pease. No other state had that. You had not only the charitable patronage but also the rich and honest and constant interest of the University. President James had himself, as you know, contributed to this series of Illinois State Historical Library publications. Dean Kinley, as he then was, and Dean Greene organized money and support, and in the case of Mr. Greene, headed various committees to increase and enlarge this contribution. So when that enormous body of source material had been brought together, there was something to work with.

In the meantime Mr. Alvord had attracted very respectful attention to Illinois in the publication of his own work, and in the organization of the Mississippi Valley Historical Association and its quarterly in 1907, of which he was the editor. That sprang almost at once to be the second periodical in history in this country, and notable among publications in its field in the world.   Of course this whole movement registered itself first within that recognized masterpiece, Mr. Alvord's account of the Mississippi Valley in the American Revolution.

Then there was gathered together support for the history itself, and for the tiny army of copyists who went over to London, Paris, Ottawa, Quebec, and elsewhere; to Albany and Worcester and New York City to gather together the source material—that is to say, copies of manuscripts.   Then the seven professors of the University and from upstate were brought in to put together this remarkable material.   And what a wonderful plan it was that Alvord laid down there, of the preliminary volume that was supposed to be distinguished from the others in being well written! But it was not, because all of them were well written—all of them were readable.   Then Mr. Alvord's beginning, and the rest down to the twentieth century.   That is not to be found elsewhere, and it excited great envy in other places.

When Dr. Flick and I schemed up our ten-volume history we wanted to do something like that which had been done in Illinois, but we could not.   In the first place, perhaps the job was too much bigger than that of Illinois, in the sense of having more people in the past to deal with, though not a more colorful history. But we lacked the support of any state university too; there isn't any in New York.   I think we lacked also a self-conscious corps of state and county historians.   We did the best we could in getting the co-operation of different chapter writers to the number of a hundred, but we have never fooled ourselves that we approached in solidity or general maturity the history that was produced by this Illinois.

Now, in closing, ladies and gentlemen, let me say that I have paid this tribute to the history and historians of Illinois simply by way of congratulating you upon the prestige of history in this state and upon the extraordinary environment in which you can work.   There is no other historical society in the United States that has its Bible laid out so conveniently as that of Illinois.   There is no place where history ought to be made vibrantly alive compared to Illinois. You have shown what a rich history you have. Now seems to me to be the time of the apostles, the time when we are to go out—I wish I could live with you at it—when we are to go out into the fields and roadsides and tell the people that this is made for them; here is knowledge that is the bread of life; here is something that makes life richer, more delightful, seemingly more useful as the individual pours out his own contribution.

The historic past of Illinois is magnificent in itself, and has been magnificently brought into a convenient shape. All that is needed now is apostolic vigor to go out into the state and tell its people that they must achieve a like level of distinction in understanding and in using history.

I have talked more than I should, but it is because I have been trapped into it by your very patient courtesy. I wish very much to thank you for this sympathetic hearing, and to congratulate you again upon the great past that presents so great an opportunity.

THE CONTRIBUTION OF THE PIONEER
PRINTERS TO ILLINOIS HISTORY

By DOUGLAS C. McMURTRIE[*]

It is a matter of especial gratification to me that we should devote this discussion to a consideration of the work of the early printers of Illinois. The services of those sturdy pioneers proved indispensable to the building of this commonwealth as well as in the recording and preservation of its written history. The services of the leading printers of those early days in Illinois deserve certainly an expression of appreciation.

In that critical period of American history following the Revolutionary War, many people, in planning their future endeavor, decided that opportunities in the East were limited. They believed that the East was overpopulated, that it was being worked out. Consequently, looking ahead, they turned their eyes across the Allegheny Mountains toward that great unsettled area which is now known as the Middle West. If we follow the records of the various trades, industries and professions, we will find that it was the young people, particularly, who plotted their futures in the western country. The men who set out for the new communities throughout the Middle West were very often men of extreme youth, just boys of nineteen or twenty-one, who turned to the frontier in the effort to make themselves homes and to build careers.

As we watch the stream of settlement into the Middle West, we find that its course was determined largely by geographic con-

---

[*] Douglas C. McMurtrie, eminent typographer and authority on the history of printing, delivered this address at the Illinois Day Meeting of the Illinois State Historical Society at Springfield, December 3, 1937.

siderations. The mountains that lay west of the Atlantic coast offered no inconsiderable barrier, so the first routes lay through the most accessible openings in those ranges. At the tiny village of Pittsburgh we find one of the most attractive gateways to the new west. Much of the stream of early settlement entered by way of Pittsburgh and continued down the Ohio River. The accessibility of the Ohio River and the ease of navigation upon it account for the fact that the southern parts of Ohio, Indiana and Illinois were settled first, leaving the northern parts of these states, in the region of the Great Lakes, to be settled at considerably later dates.

Even then, men in frontier communities were confident as to the future of the particular settlements they called home. Pittsburgh had not long been founded when a distinguished lawyer, Hugh Henry Brackenridge, decided that the city could not progress as rapidly as he had hoped unless it secured the indispensable services of a printer. Returning to Philadelphia, he persuaded two young men, John Scull and Joseph Hall, to load their printing press and types on an oxcart and travel out to Pittsburgh. Thus was the first press in Pittsburgh established in 1786. In writing of Pittsburgh in the early issues of the newspaper which he finally succeeded in having established, Brackenridge declared that this little hamlet on the frontier would become one of the great cities of the world.

Just a year later a press was carried to a more distant frontier, still deeper into the wilderness. The manner of its establishment is significant because it demonstrated the crying need for printers in the communities that were being settled throughout the "western country." This second western press was finally set up at Lexington, Kentucky, in 1787, but only at the price of considerable personal sacrifice. Kentucky was then a western county of Virginia. The region was thinly populated; settlements were sparse. But the forward-looking residents realized that, if they were to work out their own destiny in the West, they must effect a separation from Virginia and form an independent commonwealth. Delegates were elected to a convention to frame a constitution for Kentucky, but it was essential to inform the widely scattered citizens regarding its deliberations and decisions. The proceedings must be printed—but how to find a printer?

Invitations were sent to printers in North Carolina and Virginia, but to no avail. Finally a public-spirited citizen, John Bradford, a surveyor by profession, who knew nothing whatever about printing, saw an opportunity to render a great public service to Kentucky by learning the printing trade, buying a press and types, bringing the equipment to Lexington, and setting up a newspaper. He ordered a press from Philadelphia and sent his younger brother to Pittsburgh to spend a few weeks in learning the rudiments of composition. In due time the equipment arrived in Lexington, and the Bradfords brought out, in 1787, over a hundred and fifty years ago, the first issue of the *Kentucke Gazette*. This, it seems to me, was an important event in western history.

Kentucky, having grown rapidly and having shown many signs of genius in its development, had a great effect on the history of all the other territories and states in the Middle West so far as national questions were concerned. Illinois and all the other states in its category, over a great territory, looked to Kentucky in more ways than one. To confine ourselves particularly to the subject under discussion, all the states that were settled by the tide of migration down the Ohio River obtained their first printers from Kentucky.

The fast-growing town of Cincinnati, incipient metropolis of the region now constituting the state of Ohio, was the first to draw on Kentucky's typographical resources. William Maxwell responded to the local demand for a printing office and newspaper, establishing the *Centinel of the Northwestern Territory* at Cincinnati in 1793. Relatively little is known about Maxwell's origin before he moved to the West, and only within the last few years was it discovered that he first settled in Lexington, Kentucky, and did some printing there before going to Cincinnati. Apparently he found the field of printing and publishing overcrowded in Kentucky and so decided, as a second choice, to move to a town where no printer was already at work.

When the territory of Indiana was set up, the first printer appeared there in 1804. He too, as it now appears, came from Kentucky. We now know exactly whence he came and in whose office he had been working. In a communication to the Kentucky legislature, John Bradford protested against having the public printing taken away from him. As evidence of his capacity to do the work most satisfactorily, he presented, fortunately for us, a statement of the number of presses operated by, and the names of journeymen printers working for, the various printers in Kentucky. Among the journeymen printers so named was Elihu Stout, Indiana's first printer.

The next state to attract a printer from Kentucky was Missouri, which was then a part of the newly formed Louisiana Territory. When it became evident that a press would be needed at St. Louis, Joseph Charless decided to make the venture. Charless was an Irishman who sought to escape political complications in his native land by emigrating to Philadelphia. After printing in that city for several years, he moved to Lexington, Kentucky, and later to Louisville. When he decided that St. Louis might offer better opportunity, Charless, being a cautious soul, set up one press there while he still continued operation of his printing office in Louisville. In 1808, he began publication of the *Missouri Gazette* and printed laws and other public documents of the new territory. The new field proved so promising that he soon closed up his office in Kentucky and staked his future career in St. Louis.

Illinois was somewhat later than Missouri in its development, the territory being set up in 1809. Ordinarily we should expect to see a printer appear promptly; but since organization of the territory was slow, the need of a printer was not felt until it became necessary to print the laws enacted at the territory's first legislative session in 1812. But Illinois, as we know, also drew its first governor, Ninian Edwards, from Russellville, Kentucky. When the Illinois laws had to be printed and there was no printer avail-

able in the territory, Governor Edwards sent the manuscript to
Matthew Duncan, then printing at Russellville, to be put into
type. Thus, in 1813, the first Illinois statutes were printed in
Russellville, Kentucky, and the only known copy of this volume,
I believe, is preserved in the Illinois State Historical Library.[1]

The young printer in Kentucky, already favored with the
public business of Illinois Territory, naturally followed up this
advantage. Matthew Duncan moved from Russellville to Kaskaskia and became the first printer in the territory of Illinois.
At Kaskaskia be brought out the first newspaper in Illinois, the
Illinois Herald, in 1814.

What services were these pioneer printers called upon to per-
form? In the first place, when a new territory was set up, its
legislature passed certain laws. If those laws were to be effective,
and it was intended in those days that some were to be effective,
it was necessary that the judges and officers who were to admin-
ister them, as well as the population affected by them, should
know what the laws were. So one of the first acts of a territorial
government was to put the laws on record, and it was essential,
if these laws were to be given wide publicity, that they should be
printed. Thus, we find, in almost every instance, that almost
the first job of the pioneer printer to establish his press in a new
territory was the printing of laws.

In the second place, the pioneer printer always established a
newspaper. A newspaper was essential to the community, com-
mercially, as a publicity organ, and for many other purposes. In
his newspaper, also, the printer sometimes published the laws of
the United States which were of public interest. This item made
a nice addition to the printer's income, because the government
in Washington paid local newspapers for publishing the laws. And,
finally, the newspaper informed all the residents, widely scattered
throughout the territory, what was going on in the public business

---

[1] *Laws Passed by the Legislative Council & House of Representatives, of the Illinois
Territory, At their First Session held at Kaskaskia, in 1812.* The imprint on the
volume reads: "Printed by Authority from the Governor, by Matthew Duncan,
Russellville, Ky. 1813."

L A W S,

PASSED BY THE

Legislative Council & House of Repre-
sentatives,

OF THE

ILLINOIS TERRITORY,

At their FIRST SESSION held at Kaskaskia, in 1812.

Printed By Authority from the Governor,

BY MATTHEW DUNCAN,

Russellville, Ky.

1813.

TITLE PAGE OF FIRST LAWS OF ILLINOIS TERRITORY

and served to bring out for debate by the people many matters of public interest.

In other words, the newspapers, those first in each territory and those established later, provided a medium for discussion. We find that all the burning questions of the day were brought out in their columns. As the newspapers multiplied, of course, their editors took stands on one side or the other of public questions. If you will examine the early newspapers of Illinois, you will find that the one most vital issue running all through the editorial columns during the early period was the great question of slavery or free soil. I believe there was more discussion of that in Illinois than in any other neighboring state. Missouri permitted slavery, but Indiana was more or less indifferent to the subject. The severest attacks on slavery in the press, so far as the Middle West was concerned, were made in certain newspapers in Illinois. All of this must have had a great influence, in his early years, on one of our great citizens, Abraham Lincoln, foreshadowing the storm which was to come. Slavery was uppermost in the columns of the Illinois newspapers and it was, of course, the service and expression of opinion of our editors which crystallized public opinion on that great question.

But the printers not only brought out public matters in their newspapers. They also printed sermons, speeches, and other expressions of opinion in pamphlet form. They served posterity, furthermore, as well as immediate local needs, by printing the proceedings, minutes, and other records of various kinds of organizations.

The first printer in Illinois, as we have seen, was Matthew Duncan, who came from Kentucky to Kaskaskia in 1814 and founded the *Illinois Herald*. The next point of printing was Shawneetown, where the *Illinois Emigrant* was started in 1818.[2] Third was Edwardsville when, in 1819, Hooper Warren started the *Edwardsville Spectator*. The *Spectator* has significance in being

---

[2] After a two months' suspension of publication during the summer of 1819 for lack of paper, the name of the *Emigrant* was changed to *Illinois Gazette*.

the first anti-slavery organ in Illinois. The fourth point was Vandalia in 1820, and the fifth was Belleville, in 1826.

Up until this time, the spread of the press covered only the southern part of the state, which was still the destination of most of the settlers who were coming from the East. But the sixth location of the Illinois press was far to the north, at Galena, also in 1826, but after the establishment of the one at Belleville. This was not in the normal course of development, of course, but the activity in the lead mines at Galena brought an abnormal rush of people to that particular point. The establishment of a press here, out of the line of growth of the state as a whole, illustrates the fact that whenever we find a pioneer printer at work in some location far from the expected course of settlement, we also find one of two powerful influences at work. One of these is missionary zeal, and the other is the discovery of valuable mining fields.

To digress for a moment, I would briefly point out that missions devoted to christianizing the Indians brought the first press to what is now Kansas in 1834; to the present state of Oklahoma in 1835; and even to an almost inaccessible point on the Clearwater River in Idaho in 1839. Likewise, we may attribute to the influence of religious faith the first Mormon press at Salt Lake City, Utah, in 1850.

As to the effect of the discovery of precious, or at least valuable, metals I need only call attention to the influx of population which followed upon the various discoveries of gold or silver in the West. Noting the dates when gold was discovered in Colorado, in Montana, in Idaho, in South Dakota, we can estimate quite accurately when the first printer arrived in each territory. As soon as a few miners gathered in a place to start work and to establish homes, they found that they needed a newspaper. Because of such circumstances we find a press set up in Galena in 1826.

The first printing done in Springfield was the initial issue of the *Sangamo Spectator*, which appeared in 1827. A copy of this newspaper is in the Illinois State Historical Library. The next printing point in Illinois was Rock Spring, which has now disappeared from the map. But in 1829, John Mason Peck, a Baptist, founded at Rock Spring a religious publication entitled *Pioneer of the Valley of the Mississippi*, established a printing press, and there conceived and set up an educational institution which has since grown into Shurtleff College, now located at Alton.

Jacksonville, to which the first press came in 1831, became the ninth town in Illinois to receive the benefits of the press, and Alton became the tenth printing point in 1832.

Thus far, except for Galena, the growth of population and the spread of the press had all taken place in the southern half of the state. But in 1833 a press was established at Chicago, and this was significant of a new order of things. A new route of westward migration had been opened. No longer did people come to Illinois only by way of the Ohio River. The Erie Canal was completed in 1825; a new and easy means of transporting freight west as far as Buffalo had been opened up. The Great Lakes offered facilities for shipping, and we find a new stream of migration coming into the West through Buffalo and along the Great Lakes to Cleveland, Detroit, Toledo, Chicago, to say nothing of Michigan and various points in Wisconsin. With the establishment of a press at Chicago we leave this sketch of the spread of the press in Illinois.

How did these pioneer printers get along? We know that they served their communities through the printing of laws, through the transmission of news, through bringing information to interest and instruct the settlers in communities in which little reading matter was available. But how did they prosper as printers? The story is not an encouraging one. Most of the printers faced many problems. In the first place, there was the matter of financial support, of procuring subscriptions and advertisements and getting these paid for, of obtaining type, ink, and paper. Printers themselves were not any too numerous out in this new territory, so the problem of competent help was also acute. We find, for example, in the Edwardsville *Illinois Advocate*, in 1832, a note to this effect: "The Kaskaskia Democrat has finished its career." The Edwardsville editor then quoted the final address of the Kaskaskia editor:

> This number completes the second volume of the Democrat. Circumstances arising in a want of punctuality make it necessary that the press should stop, at least until we can make collections to enable us to recommence . . . . Those who are in arrears are once more requested to make immediate payment, as our necessities are urgent.

In the *Alton Spectator*, we find in 1833:

> With the present number the first volume of the Spectator ends. We had thought of suspending its publication for a few weeks in order to make some collections to enable us to free ourselves from embarrassments.

But the publisher decided to go on with the paper and hoped for the best.

Then we find an advertisement in the *Alton American* in 1834, saying that the equipment was for sale; it consisted of an iron press, type, and so forth, all nearly new, having been used only about seven months. And that was the end of the *Alton American*.

We can find abundant evidence of like situations in other printing offices. Because cash was a scarce commodity on the frontier, newspaper publishers could not often hope for payment in specie, but they could expect payment in kind, being thus supplied with some of the articles needed to live and to carry on the business. Just before Christmas, in 1831, the Edwardsville *Illinois Advocate* contained the following notice:

> This being the time for good eating and sober enjoyment, we would respectfully remind such of our subscribers as are in arrears for newspapers, job work or advertising, that their debts may be discharged in almost any of the good things of this life, from a hog down to a pound of butter or a dozen of eggs.

Up in Galena there were other products for sale. The editor of the *Miner's Journal* there announced in 1828:

> Subscriptions to this paper may be paid in lead delivered at this office; and we earnestly request those in arrears to

make immediate payment, either in cash, lead, or accepted orders on smelters.

Collections constituted only one of the publisher's ever-present worries. Even if he had cash, the printer could not always obtain paper, ink, and other supplies at the time he needed them. All through the records of these newspapers we find, every three months or so, a complaint about the difficulties in getting paper or other supplies. Thus the Galena *Miner's Journal* announced in 1828:

> We were disappointed in receiving our stock of paper from below, and consequently no paper was issued last week.

And a few months later, in January, 1829, the publisher goes to some length to explain the situation:

> It again becomes our painful duty to announce to our patrons the necessity of issuing only a half-sheet this and perhaps next week also, in consequence of a scarcity of paper. We are expecting a supply by next Monday's mail stage, however, and which should have arrived by the last. We were disappointed in the fall, at a time when it was too late to make the necessary arrangements for a winter's supply. The water had become so low that steamboats did not run from Saint Louis immediately to this place; but loading had to be un-shipped and re-shipped twice on the way.

Furthermore, we learn that the help on these early newspapers was not always as reliable as it should have been. We find this in the *Illinois Advocate* in 1831:

> We have to apologize for the non-appearance of the *Ploughboy*, this week. One of our journeymen, a member of the Temperance Society, has been so unwell as to be under the necessity of taking a certain kind of medicine, which has completely disqualified him for the duties of the office.

Also in 1831 we find the *Advocate* reporting other difficulties:

> We have issued no paper for the last two weeks owing to the excessive cold weather, and our office being too open to resist the rude attacks of the northern blast.

This recalls the case of James M. Goodhue, the first printer in St. Paul, Minnesota. When he arrived in St. Paul, he found all the buildings in great demand, but finally he obtained space in a rude shack. A frequent hindrance to his work, he reported, was occasioned by the hogs milling and rooting around under the loose boards of the floor, causing them to rise and fall.

Difficulty in getting news was another worry encountered by pioneer western printer-publishers. Strange to say, local news was all too often ignored by frontier editors. To fill their columns, they depended largely on excerpts from eastern newspapers that came to them through the mails. And since the mails were irregular and uncertain, especially in bad weather, the editors often complained that they had to omit or postpone an issue because the mail was late.

In Chicago, John Calhoun, coming from New York state, started the *Chicago Democrat* in 1833. I recently found, from a letter written earlier the same year, that John DeFrees of South Bend, Indiana, was planning to go to Chicago, and was preparing to move when he learned that Calhoun was there ahead of him. And this calls to mind another interesting story. When the Pike's Peak gold rush started in 1859, a substantial Omaha business man, William N. Byers, went out to the Pike's Peak region and satisfied himself that gold had actually been discovered there. He went back to Omaha, signed up two partners and some journeyman printers, loaded a printing outfit into an oxcart, mounted his horse, and started for Denver. At one of the supply stations along the route someone asked him where he was going with the printing press. Byers replied that he was going to the Pike's Peak gold fields. His new acquaintance then told him that another printer had passed two weeks earlier on the way to the same destination. This was not good news, so Mr. Byers hastened on ahead, leaving the oxcart to follow. At Cherry Creek (now Denver) he rented a place and laid his plans for getting out a newspaper, saying nothing to anybody about what he proposed to do. When the oxcart rolled into the settlement, Byers set up his press immediately and set about printing the first issue of his paper. Jack Merrick, who had arrived earlier, had been in no hurry about getting to work. But when he heard that there was a new press in town, he madly started to set type. A self-appointed committee of residents shuttled back and forth between the two rival printing offices to watch the race. Byers' paper, the *Rocky Mountain News*, came out twenty minutes ahead of the *Cherry Creek Pioneer*. It came out not only twenty minutes in advance, but also proved to be twice as large and twice as well edited and printed as its competitor. The publisher of the paper which appeared last gave one look at his competitor's sheet, sold his printing equipment to his rival, bought a pick and shovel, and started for the mines. It is interesting to observe that the *Rocky Mountain News* is still being published in Denver today.

Daniel H. Richards, who started the first newspaper in Milwaukee, looked over the fields at Chicago and at Milwaukee. Deciding that Chicago had no future, and that Milwaukee was going to be the metropolis of the West, he set up his publishing enterprise in the latter town.

Some of the pioneer printers settled for life in the communities they chose. But many others stayed for only a while and then moved on. We have record of at least one printer, Beriah Brown, who worked in eight different western states, all the way from his home in New York state to Washington on the Pacific Coast. He operated printing offices in the eight different states. The pioneer printers who are best known, however, are those who permanently identified themselves with the communities they elected to serve.

The more we read history and the more we look into records of one kind or another, the more we find that the only report which is really dependable is a report written on the spot where an event occurred, or very soon thereafter. History based on what people remember twenty or more years later is always subject to error and misconception. Modern methods of historical research stress the importance of contemporary records, made at the time events take place. There has thus developed, in recent years, a high respect for newspaper records. When you find in early newspaper files an account of some event written and dated at the time, you know that you are close to a first-hand statement. Historians have learned the great value of newspaper files, and considerable effort, therefore, has been devoted in recent years to locating and binding early newspapers and making them accessible for historical research. The director of the American Antiquarian Society has been spending all of his spare time for twenty-five years recording American newspapers published through 1820. From his published record scholars can ascertain the present locations of single copies and files of American newspapers earlier than 1821. And there recently has been published a union list of newspapers later than 1820, which aims to locate newspaper files all over the United States. This is a truly valuable publication.

The early printing offices issued the weekly editions of their newspapers, but they also served the public interest of their communities in other directions. For example, if there was in the community a religious organization which held annual meetings, the report of each meeting was taken to the local printer to be printed. So with fraternal organizations, Masons, Odd Fellows, and the like; such organizations had yearly and monthly meetings, and usually their yearly meetings were recorded in separate printed form. Publications of this kind, perhaps little pamphlets of only eight or twelve pages, are indispensable to the writing of local histories. And while a great deal of interest has been shown in finding newspaper files, there has been almost no effort of wide scope to find and record the locations of these other essential sources of local history.

Without going into this matter too deeply, I will say that I have been greatly concerned, for the last ten or fifteen years, in finding records of this kind, and I have been primarily interested in the light they throw on the activities of the early printers and on the printing done in particular communities. But after working on them for some time I have come also to a realization of their value as historical sources, which is more important than their worth as records of early typography.

One would think that most printed records of this character would somewhere have been preserved. It would seem plausible, for example, that a college which had been in existence for eighty years should have a complete set of its own catalogs. But it is surprising how few organizations have any continuous record of their history in the form of their own printed publications. I was once talking about early printed records with the librarian of a college in a small city in northern Illinois, and was told that the college had a full file of its catalogs, except for the years 1856 and 1857, when there was a complete break in the history of the institution. I offered to see what I could do to locate copies of the missing catalogs. It so happened that the Minnesota Historical Society was found to have copies of those two catalogs. Photostats of these copies were sent to my friend, the librarian, and the historical record of the college is now complete.

In considering Illinois history, one is impressed by the exceeding rarity of some of the early issues of the Illinois press, which are of the greatest importance from the historian's point of view. Matthew Duncan established the *Illinois Herald* in 1814. A solitary copy of one issue of that newspaper is all that can now be found. We have more printing of other kinds that Matthew Duncan did. We have, for example, the first printed message of Governor Ninian Edwards to the first Illinois territorial legislature, printed in 1814, the first year there was a press in Illinois. That message, a very valuable source of Illinois history, was owned by a gentleman living in Evanston, Illinois. When its owner died, it was put up at auction in New York and bought by a gentlemen who lives in Morristown, New Jersey. How is anyone to know that if he wishes to see the first official document printed in Illinois, he will have to go to Morristown, New Jersey?

A second piece of printing, also done at Kaskaskia by Matthew Duncan in 1814, the first year of the press, is most interesting. It

THE ILLINOIS HERALD.

BY MATTHEW DUNCAN PRINTER TO THE TERRITORY, & PUBLISHER OF THE LAWS OF THE UNION.

(Vol. I.)   Kaskaskia, Wednesday Morning, December 13, 1814.   (No. 30.)

NEW-YORK Nov. 3

By the Steam Boat, we gather from passengers, that the latest accounts from our army, General Izard still remained on the Canada side. General Brown's division only having recrossed the Niagara. Gen Drummond it would appear, had received no reinforcements as reported, and if so there may be yet more fighting in the enemy's Territory before the campaign shall finally close for the season.

Colombian.

To the Editor of the Mercury,

Buffalo, Nov. 8,

The day the province of Upper Canada was completely abandoned by the troops of the United States, and fort Erie was blown up and destroyed.

I can only remark, that the capture and defence of that place, have cost the best blood of our country. I have also immortalized the names of those who fought, who bled and died, to avenge the wrongs of an injured nation. With what honor I have been abandoned, an injured nation will judge.

P. S. The British fleet is off Niagara, a letter thirty-six hours from Utica, received by express, states there is nothing new from Sacket's Harbor.

WASHINGTON, Nov. 14.

Copy of a letter from captain Master Geringer of the United States' Sloop of War Wasp, to the Secretary of the Navy, dated, Savannah, Nov. 4, 1814.

SIR,

I have the honor to acquaint you of my arrival at this port in the British brig Atalanta, of 8 guns, prize to the U. S's. Sloop of War, Wasp, captured off the Madeira on the 21st Sept Capt. Blakeley's official despatches, will be delivered to you by Mr. R. Stewart of Philadelphia, who left L'r Orient, passenger in the Wasp. He will be detained here a day or two in order to give some testimony respecting the prize, and will immediately proceed to Washington.

The Atalanta was formerly the American brig Siro of Baltimore, captured in the Bay of Biscay, by the British sloop of War Pelican. Her cargo consists of brandy, wine, silks, fruits, &c.

I have the honor to be, your obedient servant,

D. GERINGER,

Hon. W. Jones, Secy N.

SAVANNAH, (G.) Nov. 4

Valuable Arrival
AND
Another Victory.

Arrived this forenoon, at Five Fathom Hole, the British brig Atalanta, of 258 tons, coppered to the bends with a full cargo of Wines, brandy, fruits, silks, cambricks, British bale goods, &c. prize to the U. S. ship Wasp capt. J. Blakely. The Atalanta was from Bordeaux bound to Pensacola. In coming over the bar, last night without a pilot, she went ashore on the south beach, but was soon got off, after the loss of her rudder and keel, considerably damaged.

The Atalanta was formerly the schr. Siro belonging to Baltimore, which sailed from there with a cargo of cotton for France last winter, and was captured on her passage by a British frigate.

The Wasp left L'O rient on the 27th August; five days after at 9 o'clock p. m. fell in with a British sloop of war and after an engagement of 45 minutes, she surrendered to the Wasp. Immediately after, the enemy hailed the Wasp and informed them they were in sinking condition and begged for aid; capt. Blakely was on the eve of sending his boats to her, when a second sail was descried close on board of him which compelled him to take possession of her; Mr. Geringer who was in the action on board of the Wasp, and who is prize officer on board of the Atalanta, informs us that which sheered off on the brig they engaged went down soon after with all standing; and every soul must have perished, as no assistance could be rendered her.

On the approach of the second sail she was discovered to be a brig of war, and the Wasp was to ten minutes after ready to engage her, and was in the act of wearing to do so, when two more brigs were discovered which induced capt. Blakely to make from them—they all last from...

fired a broadside into her. The Wasp which cut her rigging and did no other damage. The loss of the Wasp in this engagement was two men killed, and one slightly wounded. She received three balls in her hull, and a few in her sails and rigging.

It is supposed that the Wasp has taken, since her departure from the U. States, property to the amount of two hundred thousand pounds sterling.

The following is an extract of a letter from an officer dated,

U. States' Sloop of War Wasp, at sea, September 22, 1814.

"Besides these merchant vessels, we have whipped a of his Britannic Majesty's sloop of war, and comparatively speaking] has lost nothing. Our first engagement was with the Reindeer of 21 guns, which we whipped in 19 minutes; our loss was four killed and 23 wounded—the enemy's loss, 25 killed and 42 wounded; the greater part considered mortal.

"Our second engagement took place between 9 and night, and lasted 45 minutes, when the enemy we believe, sunk. We lost but 2 killed and 1 slightly wounded. Mr. Stewart was on board of us at the time, and will inform you of particulars."

TRURO, September, 9.

By the Lady Arabella packet, which arrived at Falmouth on Wednesday, from Lisbon, but last from Cork, we learn that about an hour before the packet left the latter place, H. M. brig Castilian, 18 guns, arrived there, having on board the Cipher, and surviving crew of H. M. late brig Avon, of 18 guns, which had sunk after a desperate action with the American ship of War Wasp, of 22 guns, (both vessels say the same, as this is false,) which sheered off on the Castillians coming up. The Avon lost 30 men in killed and wounded. The slaughter on board the Wasp was also conjectured to be very great.

THE BUBBLE BURST.

New Hampshire has already refused to join in the idle project of New England Convention, And by the following extract of a letter from a member of the Vermont Legislature, it appears

than that Vermont has repelled the proposition, with a spirit becoming a people who have recently evinced their devotion to their country.

MONTPELIER, Vt. Nov. 3.

"The Massachusetts resolutions have been before us and the committee to whom they were referred consisting of three Republicans and 3 Federalists from the Council, have unanimously reported against the adopting them and appointing delegates, and, when the report came before the House it was unanimously accepted."

Washington City, November 17.

THE NATIONAL BANK BILL.

Now before the House of Representatives, excites more than usual interest. The subject is momentous, perhaps of greater importance than any other which can come before Congress at their present session, and requires their most serious and deliberate consideration. Mr. Calhoun has made a motion going to change the whole complexion of the bill, in which we believe the House will be equally divided. In whatever way it may be decided, provided the bill shall become a law, we believe the interest of the country will be greatly subserved by it. In respect to the details of the bill, we believe no change is likely to take place, by the decision of a majority, in which those favourable to the principle of the bill ought not to acquiesce, although it may not exactly meet their views.

Wilson Cary Nicholas, is chosen Governor of the State of Virginia for the ensuing year.

COPY OF THE FIRST ILLINOIS NEWSPAPER

is a law establishing a territorial supreme court. The territorial legislature took it upon itself to create a supreme court at the same time that federally appointed judges were making up a similar court. The tribunal created by the legislature conflicted with the court made up by the federal judges, and the exchange of correspondence between the judges' supreme court and the Governor and the legislature is printed in that pamphlet of forty-five pages. I know of two copies: one in the Chicago Law Institute, and one in the State Historical Society of Missouri. The Illinois State Historical Library has a photostatic facsimile.

Let us turn for a moment to religious history. I had heard for years that there was a very extraordinary collection of Baptist material assembled by a man named Samuel Colgate and given by him to Colgate University to form a Baptist historical collection. Colgate University, better known for its football teams than for its collection of Baptist documents, is in a little town called Hamilton, in New York state. Railroad service has been discontinued to Hamilton and there is hardly a bus running there. But I had Hamilton on my schedule for a visit at the very first opportunity. Among the thousands of other valuable things I found there, were the minutes of the Crooked Creek Association of Separate Baptists, at a meeting in Schuyler County, Illinois, on November 29, 1815. The only known copy of it is there in Hamilton, New York.

And a noteworthy document of the same year is another Baptist publication of another local association, the minutes of the Illinois Association of Baptists, held at Brother David Bagley's on September 15, 1815. Like the minutes of the Crooked Creek Association, it must have been printed in Kaskaskia, as there was no other press then anywhere in Illinois. Where is this document? I am glad to report that it is within the confines of the State of Illinois. It is on a high shelf in a closet at the back of the library of Shurtleff College, at Alton. I am sure that when I went into that closet, the door had not been opened for ten years, and I am certain that nobody knew just what was to be found inside. Yet, after going through thousands of items of Baptist material, this precious document of early Illinois history was discovered.

The only known copies of the journals of the House of Representatives and of the Legislative Council of Illinois in 1817 are in the State Archives. Only one copy of each of these journals has survived the test of time. Another extremely interesting item is a catalog of the Edwardsville Library, printed in 1819. Think of a frontier library with a printed catalog in 1819. To be sure, it is a list of only some eighty books printed on one side of a sheet of paper, but it constitutes a landmark. Fortunately, the only known copy of it is carefully preserved in the Edwardsville Public Library.

And we find an address of Lewis C. Beck at the consecration of Olive Branch Masonic Lodge at Alton, Illinois, in 1823. And where must one look for this? The only known copy of it is in the Iowa Masonic Library in Cedar Rapids, Iowa. But it is not surprising to find a historical document of such importance preserved in that great Masonic collection. One must look there for many other things, too. After having looked for years for the records of Masonry in Florida Territory, I found that the only known file was in Cedar Rapids, Iowa.

The Library of Congress has the only known copy of an interesting Illinois pamphlet of 1824 on slavery. The only known copy of the bill providing for free schools in Illinois in 1825 is in the Illinois State Archives Building. We find a copy of the proceedings of the Historical Society of Illinois, at its first session in December, 1827, in the Harvard College Library in Cambridge, Massachusetts, and another copy in New York City in the library of the New York Society. The address of the president of the Historical Society at its second meeting, 1828, must be looked for in the Wisconsin Historical Society at Madison or in the Harvard College Library. The proceedings of a meeting of the citizens of Fayette County in 1831 to promote a national road are in Worcester, Massachusetts.

I have mentioned these few instances in order to emphasize

the fact that when we look for the products of the early Illinois press we cannot necessarily find them at home. In fact, one hardly knows where to begin looking for them. And this is true not only of Illinois, but of every state and community. And so it seems there is necessity for study of sources and locations of early printed material in pamphlet, book, and broadside form, just as such investigations have been made for newspaper files.

And now I should like to tell you of one of the rather important enterprises of that kind which is going on. About a year ago, I proposed to the Historical Records Survey of the Works Progress Administration, the need for a nation-wide search for early printed material throughout the country, looking for early printed documents of all the states. That project was approved, and we now have, I think, about a thousand workers in different parts of the country looking for items of historical interest of early dates and making record of them, which eventually will be made available to scholars in the historical field. There is a great number of these workers in Massachusetts, and it is my hope, if the work can continue a little longer, that we shall get a good perspective, not only of newspapers, but also of the other important work produced by our early printers.

Having envisioned some of the difficulties of these printers in getting paper for their publications, in raising money, and in accomplishing all the other feats essential to existence on the frontier, we might perhaps think that the craft of the early printer was not a particularly encouraging one. It was not. Only a few printers went on to gain some degree of wealth; others won political preferment, but this was incidental to their printing activities. Those having sufficient determination and stamina to stay with the printing and publishing enterprise earned, for the most part, small returns.

Why did they cling so tenaciously to their chosen job? Why were they willing to endure all the hardships of a pioneer printer's life? Why did they go on year after year, with very little improvement in their status? I think it was because most of these printers were idealists. They had seen, out in this western country, materials for the making of a new empire. They had caught some vision of what those little towns could some day become, and one of the important services they rendered to their communities was that of promotional salesmen.

For the frontier community could not flourish solely on its own resources. It had to be fed by new resources of men and money from the East. Thus, one of the important functions of the community's newspaper became that of sales promotion. Many western newspapers were actually subsidized by companies or individuals interested in town site promotions. It was not unusual for publishers in new settlements to print five hundred copies of their paper, though barely a hundred could be sold locally. The surplus copies were mailed "back home" by the settlers.

These papers for home circulation contained accounts, often perhaps too enthusiastic, describing the localities and telling of the advantages they offered. Many young men of ability and vigor were thus induced to leave the East, bringing their families and effects with them, to settle the West. Perhaps, if you read those early newspapers and could measure and compare their statements with the actual conditions of the time, you would almost doubt the honesty of these enthusiastic editors. They would write of a beautiful country and a city of great charm, with advantages too numerous to detail. But what they actually saw in front of them, as they wrote, was a muddy main street, full of ruts, and bordered by clumsy shacks. They would speak of fertile fields when most of the land in the neighborhood was still uncleared of stumps.

Yet in painting those pictures the writers were not, I think, intentionally dishonest. They were looking into the future and were picturing for their readers in the East visions of what those little towns on the plains would some day become. In almost every instance these visions have materialized. And the early printers who put them into type contributed in large degree to making them come true.

JOSEPH MEDILL AND THE CHICAGO TRIBUNE IN THE NOMINATION AND ELECTION OF LINCOLN

By TRACY E. STREVEY*

Located in the Northwest, in the midst of a new country endowed with vast resources and a rapidly growing population, the *Chicago Tribune*[1] occupied a strategic position. Politically the states of the Northwest were exerting an increasing influence in national affairs. Such action was often doubtful in view of the diversity of population and the settlement of large numbers of pro-southerners just north of the Ohio River. The South well realized the importance of the Northwest in the national scene and made strenuous efforts to keep the East and West divided. Any agency which could unify the Northwest or succeed in breaking the ties binding it to the Lower South was thus in a position to render southern efforts valueless. It was in this field of action that the *Chicago Tribune* played an important part. Founded in 1847, the growth of the *Tribune* was relatively slow, attended by financial difficulties, until Joseph Medill and Dr. Charles H. Ray assumed control in 1855. Other members of the *Tribune* firm at one time or another during the next ten years included John Locke Scripps, William (Deacon) Bross, Horace White and Alfred Cowles.[2] However, it was Joseph Medill who became the driving force behind the paper's growth and influence. Medill was born

* Associate Professor of History, Northwestern University.
[1] Following the consolidation of the *Tribune* with the *Daily Democratic Press* in 1858, the name was changed to the *Chicago Press and Tribune*. It appeared under this title until October 25, 1860 when it again became the *Chicago Tribune*.
[2] *Chicago Tribune*, June 10, 1897.

in Canada in 1823, but from boyhood lived on the Western Reserve of Ohio. After being admitted to the bar in 1846, Medill turned to journalism three years later, and out of this activity the *Cleveland Leader* was born.[3]

From early life Medill was possessed with a deep hatred for slavery. Although a Whig by training, he was thoroughly aroused by the failure of the Whig Party to take an anti-slavery stand in the early fifties. In 1852, Medill not only prophesied the death of the Whig Party, but through a series of articles demanded a new party and suggested the name Republican as appropriate. At a meeting in the office of the *Cleveland Leader*, held in March, 1854, an anti-slavery platform was drawn up and the name Republican adopted for the proposed party. Medill was the guiding hand in this venture and although other and more important meetings were held, his efforts in behalf of the Republican Party were significant.[4]

After Medill and Ray arrived in Chicago the prestige of the *Tribune* rapidly increased and from a sheet which was nothing more than a town gossip it became a newspaper of importance. Both men were essentially political writers and deeply interested in the growth of sentiment favoring limitation on the advancement of slavery. From the first they were active in the Republican Party of Illinois and the *Tribune* became the strongest Republican journal in the state. The editors were young men, imbued with zeal and enthusiasm, and both represented the rough nationalist school of journalists. No quarter was asked and no quarter was given in the partisan strife of those early years. From 15,000 subscribers in 1855 the number rose to 50,000 in 1860, and it was read by other thousands. A weekly edition, which represented a condensation of the daily and emphasized political and agricultural news, was circulated widely in rural areas, and Medill claimed that the people of six states regularly

[3] A. T. Andreas, *History of Chicago* (Chicago, 1885), II: 51; *Chicago Tribune*, March 17, 1899.

[4] H. I. Cleveland, "A Talk with Abraham Lincoln's Friend, the late Joseph Medill," *Saturday Evening Post*, Vol. CLXXII (Aug. 5, 1899).

read the *Tribune*.

In looking toward 1860 and a Republican victory, Medill and others wisely endeavored to aggravate the growing ill feeling between the northern and southern wings of the Democratic Party. With Douglas taking his stand on the Lecompton constitution and in opposition to the Buchanan administration, there was now a chance to break the old geographical and economic ties binding the Northwest and Lower South. The astute political leaders in the Northwest recognized the possibilities in this situation and set out to break the alliance for once and for all. According to William E. Dodd:

> No one ever saw quite so clearly as Lincoln the real meaning of this contest, and none did so much to defeat it. Without Lincoln, Douglas and Squatter Sovereignty would . . . have held those two sections together despite the extreme demands of the Lower South on the one hand and the East on the other.[5]

In this war the *Tribune* rallied to Lincoln's aid, for Medill was well aware of the situation and of the necessity for striking at the opportune moment. Taking as its guide the ideals of human liberty as opposed to the rights of propertied groups, the *Tribune* attacked the Supreme Court and mercilessly hammered its decisions. Readers were warned against the inconsistencies of slave drivers that sat on the bench.[6] Yet, with all the idealism that seemed to imbue the Republicans, their candidate had met defeat in 1858 due, in part at least, to the influence of their conservative brothers in the East. Everything seemed to point out the necessity for a return to conservatism, or at least to certain standards not too radical in nature, if they were to win in 1860. The task of the Republicans, as Medill and others saw Douglas "playing into the hands of the South in its last political campaign for national power," was to put Lincoln forward as a conservative.[7]

---

[5] William E. Dodd, "The Fight for the Northwest," *American Historical Review*, Vol. XVI, no. 4 (July, 1911), 777.

[6] *Chicago Press and Tribune*, July 29, 1858.

[7] Dodd, *Amer. Hist. Rev.*, July, 1911, pp. 784-85; see also Arthur C. Cole,

Apparently Douglas was stronger in 1859 than he had been in 1858, and Horace White, a member of the *Tribune* family, reported from the East:

> I found more Douglasism rankling in the masses of the people—especially the Democracy—than was at all pleasant to an Illinois Republican. I came to the conclusion that hardly anything short of an interposition of Providence would prevent Douglas' nomination by the Charleston Convention and his election by the people.[8]

Even while conservative reaction was in full swing and the leaders of the Republican Party were groping their way toward a program which would demand support and at the same time keep the Democracy divided, John Brown led his ill-fated expedition on Harper's Ferry. It was an embarrassing moment for a party striving to the utmost for a conservative program, and Republican papers hastened to condemn the raid as the work of an irresponsible madman.[9] The South declared such action to be the natural outcome of Republican teachings, and Douglas, speaking before Congress, placed the blame upon Republican shoulders.[10]

Medill was deeply concerned over the political effects of Harper's Ferry and wrote Chase:

> I very much fear that old Brown has furnished the un-horsed Democracy with ammunition to renew the fight and that our party will suffer in the eyes of the conservative class.

"President Lincoln and the Illinois Radical Republicans," *Mississippi Valley Historical Review*, Vol. IV, no. 4 (March, 1918), 418-20. "In certain sections of the state the republican party had still to assume the guise of a 'People's Party,' lest it should frighten off the more conservative voters who might wish to support candidates. . . . It was still possible to keep voters from supporting party nominees . . . . on the ground that these candidates were abolitionists.

"In the campaign of 1860 [Lincoln's] claims were pushed as those of a conservative republican standing substantially on Henry Clay ground. Again and again did he repeat the republican guarantee to the institution of slavery in the southern states where it already existed."

[8] Horace White to Trumbull, Dec. 8, 1858 (Trumbull MSS, Library of Congress).

[9] *Illinois State Journal*, Oct. 22, 1859.

[10] Allen Johnson, *Stephen A. Douglas: A Study in American Politics* (New York, 1908), 414.

I would not be greatly surprised if we lose New York and New Jersey next week as the first fruits of Harper's Ferry, and perhaps Wisconsin also. . . . A vast number of our people are emigrants from slave states and you can hardly imagine the effect produced on their minds by the idea of negro stealing or negro insurrection. It has killed Seward stone dead as the revelations now stand. It is a terrible blow and throws our party on the defensive. We will eventually outlive it and throw off the taint sought to be fastened upon us; but in the meantime we will lose part of the pounds recently gained. Its effect may be felt even on the Presidential election. Another injury is that it will scare off the Southern opposition who were rapidly taking ground and forming in our rear to march by a flank movement against the Democracy. The Southern opposition had undoubtedly made up their minds to act as our allies next year. But the pressure of alarm and democratic clamor may compel them to resume a hostile attitude toward us.[11]

The Republicans, thus thrown on the defensive at a time when they were already losing some ground, met the assaults of the Democrats in a dignified manner, stating that "their party had no intention of interfering with slavery in the States and condemning the raid at Harper's Ferry."[12] John Brown was pictured as a misguided champion of slavery for whose action the party could not bear responsibility. Such a fanatical expedition was held to be entirely outside the aims and purposes of the Republican organization, hence it could not be blamed for something of which it was innocent.

The position of the Republicans in 1859-1860 was far removed from that of Lincoln's "House Divided" speech, and Lincoln, the sometime radical, was swept along on the wave of conservatism. Radicalism meant defeat, conservatism meant availability, and both meant victory for the Republicans. That much was clear to the party leaders of Illinois, for had not the Republican vote remained almost stationary from 1856 to 1858 and this in the face

---

[11] Medill to Chase, Oct. 30, 1859 (Chase MSS, Library of Congress; others in Pennsylvania State Historical Society).

[12] James Ford Rhodes, *History of the United States* (New York, 1893), II: 402.

of a heavy foreign influx?[13]

The possibility of Abraham Lincoln as the presidential candidate of the Republican Party in 1860 was no doubt considered by some as early as the time of his "lost speech" in 1856. Without question, he had then become a leader of his party in the West, but it remained for the Lincoln-Douglas debates to create sufficient enthusiasm to warrant his serious consideration.

Once brought into the limelight, Lincoln carried on an offensive campaign against Douglas as the "Little Giant" journeyed up and down the land trying to extricate himself from the fatal trap sprung at Freeport. His record was attacked, and in Ohio in the fall of 1859 Lincoln made the point that the doctrine of unfriendly legislation meant that a thing may be lawfully driven away from where it has a lawful right to stay.[14] Douglas was shown to be playing both ends against the middle and, although Lincoln was not in a real sense a national figure, he was fast coming to the attention of the people. His stock had boomed in Illinois when Seward and others in the East had looked askance at his election for senator, and the independent-thinking Republican of the western state was determined to push Lincoln into the highest office of the land if only to show the East that Seward could not get the nomination.

Thus all through the year 1859, men were at work making plans and laying the foundation of an efficient party organization which would carry Lincoln to the convention.[15] In the spring of that year, the Republican State Committee met in the office of the *Tribune*, where a definite scheme for booming Lincoln was concocted. Medill reported that the press downstate, particularly in the old Whig belt, was to broach the subject, then a Springfield paper would take it up, then another farther north—"say in Rock Island"—until the boom should reach Chicago.[16]

---

[13] Dodd, *Amer. Hist. Rev.*, July, 1911, pp. 784-88.
[14] *Chicago Press and Tribune*, Oct. 6, 1859; Daniel J. Ryan, "Lincoln and Ohio," *Ohio Archaeological and Historical Quarterly*, Vol. XXXII, no. 1 (Jan. 1923), 86.
[15] Ida M. Tarbell, *The Life of Lincoln* (New York, 1908), II: 131.
[16] Cleveland, *Sat. Eve. Post*, Aug. 5, 1899.

The committee and leading Republicans of the state believed it advisable to keep Lincoln in the background as long as possible before pushing his claims on a national scale. It was thought the friends of Seward, Bates, Cameron, and Chase would fight each other, while Lincoln, being out of the struggle, would remain undamaged and at the proper time could be brought forward.[17]

About the middle of December, 1859, Medill went to Washington, ostensibly as a correspondent for the *Tribune*, but in reality to sound eastern opinion and promote Lincoln's nomination. He wrote of his experiences there:

> We were not rich and my office was under my hat. I stopped at Willards where were John A. Bingham of Ohio and Hannibal Hamlin. Before writing any Lincoln letters for the "Tribune" I began preaching Lincoln among the Congressmen. I urged him chiefly upon the ground of availability in the close and doubtful States, with what seemed like reasonable success.[18]

Yet it is clear that, earlier in the same year, Medill had not made up his mind that Lincoln was a better western candidate than Chase of Ohio. Although there was nothing in the *Press and Tribune* to indicate this frame of mind, his correspondence shows otherwise. There is little doubt that Medill thought Chase stood a better chance in the convention than did Lincoln, and for several months the Chicago editor was engaged in wirepulling and manipulations for Chase. Following a talk with Colfax at the Richmond House in Chicago, Medill wrote Chase:

> We compared notes freely and I think I have won him over to your side. He admitted that Chase and Bell would make a formidable ticket. He suggested you and Bates. I learn that the *Cincinnati Gazette* is for Chase and Bates but Bell would be stronger if he would accept. But if Bates could be worked up a little higher and would take the Vice-Presidency he would keep the ticket in the West. Colfax was fearful that

---

[17] *Memoirs of Gustave Koerner, 1809-1896*, edited by Thomas F. McCormack (Cedar Rapids, Iowa, 1909), II: 80.

[18] *Chicago Press and Tribune*, Feb. 16, 1860; Tarbell, *Life of Lincoln*, II: 133.

Seward's friends would control the convention and nominate him.[19]

In regard to his own policy, Medill wrote Chase:

Before long I propose to write one or more leading articles in favor of nominating a Western Candidate without espousing the claims of any man or of attacking Seward. We do not think it policy thus early to commit our paper publicly to any candidate, but to work underground for you and openly for a western man. The moment we take sides in our columns for you it will be a signal for the Seward organs to make a fight against you. We must not fire the mine until the powder is properly laid, else there may be a premature explosion that will do more harm than good. I hope you will concur in these present views.[20]

In the summer of 1859, Medill attended the Republican convention at St. Paul where he found Joseph Hoxie of New York laying wire for Seward. At the same time he was encouraged by the sentiment expressed for Chase, which he thought could be enhanced if Chase would take a definite stand on the tariff. In writing to Chase, Medill stated:

By the way, I really think it will be necessary for you to define your position on that subject. Nobody is in favor of a high protective tariff or prohibitive tariff. But the present one is ruinous. It is taxation without even incidental protection. There must be a change, the country will not receive, will not enjoy solid safe prosperity until we supply more of our own wants and import less from abroad of those staples which we can so well make at home.[21]

In the same letter Medill advised Chase to remove the objection that he was a free trader by taking a sound stand on the tariff issue.

As the political situation became intensified and more candidates loomed in the North as possible selections for the Republican

---

[19] Medill to Chase, April 26, 1859, Chase MSS.
[20] Medill to Chase, June 8, 1859, *ibid*.
[21] Medill to Chase, June 27, 1859, *ibid*.

Party, Medill expressed himself regarding several of these in no uncertain terms. He looked upon Bates as a "very nice man," but he declared further:

> He has not said and dare not say that the constitution recognizes no property in man, that the common law recognizes none and that the general government must recognize none. That's our position. Whenever we fall below it we sink into the quicksands and will soon disappear. Let us be beaten by a representative man rather than triumph with a "Union Saver."[22]

Chase was warned by Medill in August, 1859, that Bates was strong in central and southern Illinois and in certain parts of Iowa. With Frank Blair sowing Bates seed in New England and New York and the rumor floating about that Bates would take a "right and safe" stand on slavery, Medill thought him the most formidable opponent Chase would face.[23] As for Seward, Medill wrote:

> I think Seward's chances have been growing smaller by degrees for six months past; every day's reflection and discussion by members of the party go to show them that he is not available. If Bates does not get in your way, I consider you [Chase] have a pretty sure thing of the nomination, but he may be so pushed and trained by the Blairs as to divide your western strength. This is my chief fear.[24]

A month later, Medill again urged Chase to place himself right on the tariff issue and declared that Lincoln was rapidly forging ahead as a prospective candidate in Illinois and Indiana. Chase did try to controvert the impression that he was a free trader by denying such an accusation implicitly and asking his friends in the East and West to silence the opposition on that ground. Medill meanwhile seems to have been swept along with the growing enthusiasm for Lincoln and by late fall was fully committed to the Illinois "Rail Splitter."

---

[22] Letter quoted in Ovando J. Hollister, *Life of Schuyler Colfax* (New York, 1886), 125.
[23] Medill to Chase, Aug. 30, 1859, Chase MSS.
[24] *Ibid.*

Following Medill's journey to the capital where public opinion was sounded by the astute politician from the West, the *Tribune* came out editorially for Lincoln on February 16, and the boom was on. Bearing the caption, "The Presidency—Abraham Lincoln," a third of the editorial dealt with the general political condition of the nation and the latter part presented Lincoln's claims in several numbered paragraphs:

1st. A gentleman of unimpeachable purity of private life. His good name is not soiled by a single act, political, social, moral or religious, that we or his friends need blush to own as his. In all of his relations to his fellows he has not yet been guilty of that thing upon which an enemy can place a finger and say, "This is dishonest," or "This is mean." Herein he is the peer of the most unspotted man of the Republic—the living likeness, full length size, of the best of the eminent characters who laid the foundation of the government.

2nd. A man of, at once, great breadth and great acuteness of intellect. Not learned in a bookish sense, but master of great fundamental principles, and of that kind of ability which applies them to crises and events. The masterly canvass which he made with Douglas, and his later speeches in Ohio, mark him as one of the ablest political thinkers of his day.

3rd. Right on the record. An old line Whig acceptable to Pennsylvania and New Jersey—candidate of the party which in itself is an embodiment of the principles and measures necessary for the perpetuity of the Union and the preservation of our free institutions—he would enter the field acceptable to the Opposition of all shades of opinion, harmonizing all interests, conciliating all jarring elements, a guarantor of success.[25]

Medill followed this editorial with a letter from Washington in which Lincoln was named as a candidate on whom both conservative and radical sentiment could unite, and declaring that he now heard Lincoln's name mentioned for president in Washington ten times as often as it was a month earlier.[26] It was a

---

[25] *Chicago Press and Tribune,* Feb. 16, 1860.
[26] Tarbell, *Life of Lincoln,* II: 133; *Chicago Press and Tribune,* Feb. 26, 1860.

ringing plea for Lincoln, and Medill claimed it as the first east of the Alleghenies to point out the availability of the Illinois candidate.[27]

When the *Chicago Tribune* arrived in Washington bearing in its columns the letter by Medill, the friends of Seward proceeded to "jump on" the *Tribune* editor. Medill related that while at a reception given for the British Minister, Seward took advantage of the occasion and "blew him up." The New York leader said to Medill:

> You have stunned me. I've read that letter in which you advocate Lincoln for the Presidency in preference to me, giving reasons that are wide of the truth, saying I haven't the strength Lincoln has and would be defeated as Fremont was and that your man out there on the prairies can carry the essential states. Do you mean that?

After Medill assured him that he did, Seward continued:

> I consider this as a personal insult. I had always counted on you as one of my boys. Henceforth you and I are parted. The golden chain is broken. I defy you to do your worst. I know three papers in your town that are with me and I shall never trust you again.[28]

Medill had known Seward as early as 1848 and in some respects looked upon him as his *"beau idéal"* of a statesman and a valued political mentor.[29] But Medill, in looking for availability, had reached the conclusion by 1860 that Seward could carry neither Illinois, Indiana, nor Pennsylvania, and without their electoral vote would come no nearer being elected than Fremont did in 1856. He believed Seward to be radical on the slavery question when radicalism should be cast aside. The "irrepressible" doctrine was too much for the conservatives to swallow, and Medill thought that Lincoln, a Kentuckian by birth, could carry

---

[27] Cleveland, *Sat. Eve. Post*, Aug. 5, 1899.
[28] *Ibid.*
[29] Frederic Bancroft, *The Life of William H. Seward* (New York and London, 1900), I: 530n.

those states and, in addition, all those Fremont had swept four years earlier.

Medill further claimed:

> [Seward] proceeded to declare, with much heat of temper and expression, that if he was not nominated as the Republican candidate for President at the ensuing convention, he would shake the dust off his shoes, and retire from the service of an ungrateful party for the remainder of his days. . . . He gave me to understand that he was the chief teacher of the principles of the Republican Party before Lincoln was known other than as a country lawyer of Illinois.[30]

While Dr. Ray managed the *Tribune*, Medill kept on writing from Washington. His letters were carried in full and can be found scattered through the issues of the *Tribune* during February and March. He encouraged Lincoln to consider nothing except the presidency for, as he explained, "When you go to a theatre always buy a box ticket, because with that you can sit anywhere but if you buy a pit ticket you must sit in the pit or go out." He reasoned that it was better to aim high, for if Lincoln had to "come down a peg" later on, the Seward faction would be eager to give him at least the vice-presidency. Until that time, it was the presidency or nothing.[31]

Meanwhile the Republican leaders of Illinois, after carefully analyzing the situation, realized full well the value of having the National Convention in the West, and more particularly amidst the vociferous partisans of Lincoln. It was decided that Norman B. Judd of Chicago, then a member of the National Committee, should urge the selection of Chicago as the home of the convention on the basis that it was neutral ground. When the choice was finally made as the Illinois Republicans desired, the first step toward the nomination of Lincoln had been taken.[32]

The state committee likewise arranged for Lincoln to extend

---

[30] Bancroft, *Life of Seward*, I: 531n. Medill stated, of his reply to Seward, that "it had none of the tendency of oil poured on stormy water."

[31] Cleveland, *Sat. Eve. Post*, Aug. 5, 1899.

[32] Koerner, *Memoirs*, II: 80.

his campaign into the Seward stronghold. It was necessary for him to become a national figure before the convention met, and at the same time to put at rest the eastern conception of his radicalism. On his way to New York, where he was to deliver a speech at the Cooper Union Institute, Lincoln dropped into the office of the *Chicago Tribune* and held a brief conference with Medill and Ray. He mentioned the fact that he was to face a critical and partisan audience and requested that the two publishers read and criticize his speech for grammatical errors, but not the arguments as they would have to stand. Ray and Medill sat far into the night reading and making notations where the construction could be improved, and it was with a self-satisfied feeling that the manuscript was returned to Lincoln the following morning.[33] When the report of the Cooper Union speech reached Chicago, it was found that Lincoln had used few of the suggestions,[34] for as Medill said, "Lincoln usually had his mind made up and was a hard man to swerve."

Lincoln, holding true to the need of appearing conservative in the East, founded his utterances at Cooper Union on the Constitution and the Fathers. He showed that the Fathers held and acted upon the conception that Congress had power to regulate slavery in the territories, and that the Republican Party was a conservative party for it maintained this doctrine of the Fathers. Furthermore, Lincoln pointed out that it was the South who refused to abide by the policy of the makers of the Constitution, and at all hazards they meant to rule or ruin.[35] He was essentially a conservative and was careful not to base his doctrine on the Jeffersonian conception "that all men are created free and equal."[36] He did not repeat his "House Divided" theory but instead declared: "Wrong as we think slavery is, we can yet afford to let it alone where it is, because that much is due to the necessity

---

[33] Cleveland, *Sat. Eve. Post*, Aug. 5, 1899; Carl Sandburg, *Abraham Lincoln: The Prairie Years* (New York, 1926), II: 210.
[34] Sandburg, *The Prairie Years*, II: 215-16.
[35] Rhodes, *History of the United States*, II: 431-32.
[36] Dodd, *Amer. Hist. Rev.*, July, 1911, p. 785.

arising from its actual presence in the nation."[37]   His attitude was such that the radicals of Illinois condemned his speech and Lincoln himself did not greatly blame them.

Paralleling this development, a city election campaign was being carried on in Chicago and intense rivalry was evidenced between the Republicans and Democrats.   Medill thought the situation serious enough to warrant an open letter for all voters to read, especially in view of the coming convention.   From Washington he wrote:

> From the report sent here by the Douglas men, some of our folks begin to fear that through disaffection among the Republicans, the bogus Democrats will carry Chicago.   This idea gives them cold chills.   Senator Wilson says the loss of Chicago at this crisis will endanger Connecticut and do much to ensure the nomination of Douglas at Charleston.   At least thirty members of Congress from other states have spoken to me about it.   They say that for the cause and the great campaign the city must be saved.
>
> Wade, Senator from Ohio, told me that the loss of Chicago would be the worst blow that the Republican Party could now receive.   He says he is ready to go there and stump every ward to save it.   This is the general feeling.   A National Convention is soon coming off and great things are expected at Chicago.   She is the pet Republican city of the Union—the point from which radiate opinions which influence six states.[38]

The *Tribune* urged every reader to put this letter in his pipe and smoke it.   It demanded that in the face of such explicit testimony it was the duty of all men to "up and at 'em."[39]   Evidently the voters did "up and at 'em" for early in March the *Tribune* enthusiastically announced a Republican victory under such glowing captions as, "First Gun for 1860," "1,400 Republican Majority," "Douglas Dead as a Smelt," "The Tipperary Men Cleaned out," and "Great Republican Carnival."[40]

---

[37] Rhodes, *History of the United States*, II: 432.
[38] *Chicago Press and Tribune*, Feb. 29, 1860.
[39] *Ibid.*
[40] *Ibid.*, March 7, 1860.

According to the *Chicago Tribune*, the Republican Party as a political organization had nothing to do with the question of abolishing slavery or bettering the conditions of the slaves. Its action affecting or intended to affect the institution of slavery was claimed to be repressive only. It sought to prevent its increase by opposing the reopening of the African slave trade and to curtail its political power in the general government by opposing the introduction of slavery into the territories. It was not denied that such a platform would to some extent aid in the abolition of slavery.[41]

The platform, as laid down by the *Tribune* in March, 1860, for the consideration of the convention, contained the following points:

1. To preserve the Territories to freedom and free labor, to prevent the monopoly of their soil by the owners of slave labor, to save free labor from degradation which always follows contact with slavery, and to secure the best of schools, universities and churches without which a high degree of intelligence, morality and thrift is entirely impossible.

2. To give the lands to the landless and to encourage settlers from both the free and slave states to enter upon our unsettled domain by the free gift of the homestead.

3. To strengthen the political power in the national government of the white laborers, by rapidly building up new free states and thus placing the representatives of the slavery oligarchy in our national councils in a hopeless minority.

4. To make such revisions of the financial policy of the government as will result in protecting the free white labor of this country from ruinous competition with the pauper labor in Europe, and which will assure a home market for our agricultural staples.

5. Reciprocal free trade with all governments of the new world and the development of an American policy to link them closer together by a community of interests.

6. Improvement of our rivers and harbors and the construction of a Pacific railroad, cheapening the carriage of all articles of commerce, and facilitating intercourse between

---

[41] *Chicago Press and Tribune*, March 1, 1860.

all parts of our widely extended confederacy.[42]

In the issues of the *Tribune* leading up to the Republican Convention, one finds, in almost every edition, articles and editorials dealing with the problems facing the party. The political condition of the country at large was carefully analyzed in order that the people might realize the responsibility resting upon all members of the party. The fight for Republican supremacy was carried openly to the public and all were warned that a candidate must be selected by the convention who could carry the doubtful states.[43]

It brought out that Lincoln's record, both political and personal, was without a line or blemish for which any Republican need be ashamed. Lincoln's course as a member of the Illinois legislature or as a member of the House of Representatives, was declared to be above reproach. According to the *Tribune*, his growth in anti-slavery sentiment was not the result of any "quickening hothouse process, but the ripening of his convictions."[44]

His work for the Republican cause was emphasized and it was pointed out that "perhaps no other man in the nation has made as many speeches in support of the distinctive principles of the Republican Party as Abe Lincoln."[45] His time and effort were given freely, so why not support him, asked the *Tribune*.

By March 10, 1860, the *Tribune* had arrived at the conclusion that to nominate Lincoln, Seward would have to be overcome, since the strength of the East seemed to be centered on the New Yorker. As one issue stated:

> We have long believed and still believe that the real struggle is between Seward and Lincoln, and that one or the other will be selected for the chief honor which the convention has to bestow, and the success of the latter we frankly admit depends upon the real or supposed want of availability of the former. It is not probable that in any contingency the con-

[42] *Chicago Press and Tribune*, March 1, 1860.
[43] *Ibid.*, March, April, May, 1860.
[44] *Ibid.*, March 1, 1860.
[45] *Ibid.*, March 2, 1860.

vention will go outside the party for its candidate; if not, the question of availability must be discussed and settled on the spot.[46]

In reply to an article in the *Illinois State Register* stating that Lincoln had better judgment than to allow his friends to set him up on a pinnacle from which he was sure to be knocked down, the *Tribune* answered:

He is our candidate and will remain so until the convention takes away our right to support him as partisans. If the *Journal* thinks differently, we shall agree to disagree. That's all.[47]

By the end of March, the editorials changed somewhat and became stronger in tone. They took more the aspect of a call to unite on the one man available to all groups.

If the members of the Republican Party could be induced to forego their personal preferences and nominate a man for the Presidency to whom both principle and expediency point, Mr. Lincoln would be put at the head of the ticket by acclamation. . . . We know nothing but unwise adherence to the personal fortunes of other candidates in the convention that will defeat his nomination. Certainly the friends of Seward, Chase and Bates may meet upon him and all can be assured that in him each can find the qualities which command approbation in the candidate of his first choice.[48]

The *Tribune*, in casting about for political weapons, played up the idea that if Douglas were nominated at Charleston, there was no other man in the country besides Lincoln who stood a chance of winning the election. The fact that Lincoln had met and vanquished Douglas in the series of debates, even though losing the election by a close margin, was impressed upon the public as sufficient evidence in his favor.

As the time drew near for the Illinois State Convention which was to meet in Decatur on May 9, Lincoln workers redoubled

---

[46] *Chicago Press and Tribune*, March 10, 1860.
[47] *Ibid.*, March 15, 1860.
[48] *Ibid.*, March 22, 1860.

their efforts. They realized that all their labor would amount to little if their own convention did not nominate Lincoln as its first choice. Seward possessed considerable strength in the northern counties and in Chicago, but the majority of the others were almost unanimous for Lincoln.[49] By April, the Lincoln standard was raised far and wide over the state and it was a foregone conclusion that the convention could do no less than put Abraham Lincoln forward as its choice for the presidency.[50]

On the day the Republican delegates were gathering in Chicago, the *Tribune* formally announced Lincoln as its candidate and the candidate of Illinois. In a series of articles extending over May 15 and 16, the *Tribune* listed the following points in his favor:

1. By his own choice Lincoln is not a candidate. He never sought directly or indirectly for the first or second place on the ticket. The movement for him was entirely spontaneous and he would enter the contest with no clogs or embarrassments, this fact alone constituting a guaranty of a glorious triumph.

2. "In all the fundamentals of Republicanism he is a radical up to the limit to which the party with due respects to the rights of the South propose to go."

3. "Lincoln is not striving for nor has a record to make." Originally a Whig, he has no explanations to make and his position on the tariff is guaranteed as acceptable to all Republicans.

4. "Lincoln is a Southern man by birth and education."

5. Mr. Lincoln is a man of the people. "For his position he is not indebted to family influence, partiality of friends, or the acts of a politician." The fact that he was a laborer in his early life, in the fields, in the sawmill, and a boatman on the great rivers, was emphasized in order to show his sympathy for those who toiled.

---

[49] John G. Nicolay and John Hay, *Abraham Lincoln: A History* (New York, 1890), II: 259; William E. Barton, *The Life of Abraham Lincoln* (Indianapolis, 1925), I: 413.

[50] *Chicago Press and Tribune*, April-March, 1860; Koerner wrote that the German population preferred Seward but would vote for Lincoln at the proper time. Koerner to Trumbull, March 15, 1860, Trumbull MSS.

6. "He is without a stain of Know-Nothingism, he is acceptable to the great mass of American voters who will be compelled to choose between the candidate of Chicago and the Democratic nominee."

7. "Mr. Lincoln is an honest man."

8. The *Tribune* concluded, "We need not add that Mr. Lincoln can be elected if placed before the people with the approbation of the convention which meets tomorrow."[51]

From a preliminary survey of the existing conditions, facts seemed to indicate that the fight for the nomination was Seward against the field. Backed by a strong delegation and a great body of "rooters" led by the redoubtable Tom Hyer of pugilistic fame, the Seward crowd determined to overcome all opposition. Called the "Irrepressibles," they acted the part and with bands and shouting the "rooters" paraded the streets.[52] At the outset, everything pointed toward Seward, and on trains coming into Chicago straw votes gave Seward a tremendous lead over the other prospective candidates and, in particular, over Lincoln.[53]

The outlook for Seward was increasingly rosy as his opposition seemed divided between Chase, Bates, Cameron, Lincoln and Wade.[54] The problem facing the Illinois delegation was to unite this opposition on Lincoln, and to accomplish as much as possible before the convention formally convened. Lincoln's friends felt he could be elected if nominated and the nomination must therefore be secured.[55] Making their headquarters at the Tremont House some five blocks from the Wigwam, David Davis,Stephen T. Logan, Leonard Swett, Norman B. Judd, George Schneider, I. N. Arnold, Medill, Ray, and others worked "like nailers."[56]

---

[51] *Chicago Press and Tribune*, May 15, May 16, 1860.

[52] Murat Halstead, *Caucuses of 1860: A History of the National Political Conventions* (Columbus, 1860), 120-54.

[53] Barton, *Life of Lincoln*, I: 426.

[54] H. Freisman to Washburne, May 16, 1860, Washburne MSS (Library of Congress); Halstead, *Caucuses of 1860*, 140-41.

[55] Hollister, *Colfax*, 147.

[56] Koerner, *Memoirs*, II: 85; Joseph Fort Newton, *Lincoln and Herndon* (Cedar Rapids, Iowa, 1910), 272.

There, plans were made and a "political huckster shop" was opened, for it was soon evident that dickering for votes would be an important and necessary procedure.[57]

The two doubtful states, Indiana and Pennsylvania, were necessary to the success of the plans of Lincoln's managers, and pressure was applied where it would do the most good. Medill reported that half the Indiana delegation had been won over to Lincoln on the ground of availability even before the convention opened.[58] There is little question that promises were made to Indiana, Ohio, and Pennsylvania for their support of Lincoln, even though Lincoln, remaining in Springfield, had warned his friends against such action. Ray reported to Medill at the Tremont House that Indiana was nailed down and would vote solid for Lincoln on the first ballot, stating that "By the Lord, we promised them everything they asked."[59]

As for Pennsylvania, with its huge block of votes, Medill wanted the big Pennsylvania foot brought down hard on the Lincoln scale. Lincoln was informed by telegraph that the Cameron contingent could be secured if the Pennsylvanian were promised a cabinet position but in reply stated decisively that he would not be bound by any contract or bargain.

> Everybody was mad, of course. . . . What was to be done? The bluff Dubois said: "Damn Lincoln." The polished Swett said, in mellifluous accents: "I am very sure if Lincoln was aware of the necessities—" The critical Logan expectorated viciously, and said, "The main difficulty with Lincoln is—" Herndon ventured: "Now, friend, I'll answer that." But Davis cut the Gordian knot by brushing all aside with: "Lincoln ain't here, and don't know what we have to meet, so we will go ahead, as if we hadn't heard from him and he must ratify it."[60]

In Medill's account, he stated that after the Illinois delegates

---

[57] Newton, *Lincoln and Herndon*, 272.
[58] Sandburg, *The Prairie Years*, II: 341-42; Tarbell, *Life of Lincoln*, II: 141.
[59] Sandburg, *The Prairie Years*, 341.
[60] Newton, *Lincoln and Herndon*, 273, quoting from W. C. Whitney, *Life of Lincoln*, 289.

Chicago Wigwam, 1860

had gone to sound out the Pennsylvania group, he waited in the Tremont House for the final word. About midnight, Judge Davis came down the stairs and told Medill, "Damned if we haven't got them." To the query "how" was returned the answer, "By paying their price." Ray, who had been in attendance at the conference, told Medill that Cameron had been promised a cabinet position, remarking that such was a small price when playing for the presidency.[61]

One figure at the convention who aided in the break-up of the Seward machine was the eccentric editor of the *New York Tribune*. Hating Seward and determined to blast his hopes of the nomination, Greeley secured a place in the convention as a substitute delegate from Oregon. Flitting here and there, from caucus to caucus, he let it be known that it would be disastrous to the future security of the party if Seward were nominated. Although he considered Lincoln as an outsider and not within the pale of possibility, yet Greeley did without question aid in the building up of an anti-Seward combine.[62] Bates was his first choice as a "safer" man and one upon whom all the Republicans could rally.

In the seating of the delegates, the arrangements were in charge of Medill and Norman Judd. Medill relates that in carrying this out:

> New York was for Seward and the isolation of its delegates was desired by the Lincoln men. Pennsylvania was the most important doubtful state. It followed that the New York delegates were seated at one end of the vast hall with no state for neighbor that was not hopelessly for Seward. At the other end of the hall where the voices of the Seward orators could hardly be heard was placed Pennsylvania. Between Pennsylvania and New York were placed the Illinois delegates and also those of Indiana and New Jersey.[63]

---

[61] C. S. Pike, *First Blows of the Civil War* (New York, 1879), 519; Sandburg, *The Prairie Years*, II: 342.

[62] L. D. Ingersoll, *The Life of Horace Greeley* (Chicago, 1873), 338.

[63] Cleveland, *Sat. Eve. Post*, Aug. 5, 1899.

Medill believed to the last that this arrangement had a great influence in weakening the power of Seward as it removed pressure which otherwise might have been applied to the doubtful states.

It was likewise arranged that tickets of admittance to the Wigwam should be given to Illinoisans in preference to those of other states. The plans were to fill the hall with vociferous Lincoln "shouters" and exclude as many followers of Seward as possible. Judd had fixed it with the railroads to bring in Lincoln men free of charge and the city teemed with those carrying Lincoln "Rails." On the night preceding the session of the convention which would determine who was to lead the party in its campaign for victory, men sat far into the small hours making out tickets and these were distributed by the hundred to Lincoln followers. Instructions were to report early to the Wigwam and jam it to the doors. As a result of the activity of these men, the Seward "Irrepressibles" found many of their number excluded from the hall on the morning of the third day.[64]

Following the formal nominations of the candidates, it was seen that the struggle lay between Lincoln and Seward. Two hundred and thirty-three votes constituted a majority. Could Lincoln win? On the first ballot, Seward received 173½ votes; Lincoln, 102; Cameron, 50½; Chase, 49; and Bates, 48.[65] Meanwhile the Illinois delegation, fearing the strength of Ohio which might be swung to Seward, sent Medill to sit among his old friends. In his own words:

> I took my seat among my old friends of the Ohio delegation, but Joshua Giddings without ceremony ordered me out. My friends came to my rescue, we had a nice little argument and I stayed. After the second ballot I whispered to Carter of Ohio, "If you can throw the Ohio delegation for Lincoln, Chase can have anything he wants." "H-how d'dye know?" stuttered Carter. "I know and you know or I wouldn't promise if I didn't know." So Carter got up and announced 18 or 19 votes of Ohio for Lincoln but on the poll it was found

[64] Koerner, *Memoirs*, II: 85.
[65] Rhodes, *History of the United States*, II: 469; Halstead, *Caucuses of 1860* 143-50.

that Carter hadn't nigged more than one or two votes. That settled the nomination for Lincoln.[66]

On the morning after the nomination the *Tribune* appeared bearing this editorial on Lincoln:

> No other man in the nation stands so near the popular heart today; and in the exigencies to which corrupt rulers have brought our government, and amid the perils which on every hand threaten our free institutions, the people turn instinctively to him as the man for the occasion—as one who has been led by Providence through all the experiences of lowly life, through labor and privation, through struggles and sacrifices, into self-reliance, into honest simplicity of life, into nobleness and purity of character, into a love of justice, of truth, and freedom, that he might be fitted for his work.[67]

Certain eastern newspapers described the Lincoln victory in the convention as an accident and claimed it was only through Horace Greeley that he was nominated. In fact, the whole thing was rather strange and it was inferred that the nomination was not altogether above suspicion. Eagerly the *Tribune* answered these innuendoes, tersely stating:

> It is the stupidest blunder into which a dozen or more responsible newspapers could possible have fallen. The truth is Mr. Greeley opposed Lincoln down to the last moment with just as much earnestness as he opposed Seward, and Mr. Thurlow Weed, though working industriously no doubt, failed so far as we know to win a single vote. In spite of his labor a large number of delegates who came here under a quasi-pledge to Seward were taken out of his hand and on the third ballot carried over to Lincoln. We think it may be difficult to pick out two men of equal strength or standing with the party who were in the convention as weak as these men proved to be. Greeley had no weight with the straight Republicans in consequence of his committal to Bates and Mr. Weed was just as powerless.[68]

---

[66] Cleveland, *Sat. Eve. Post*, Aug. 5, 1899.
[67] *Chicago Press and Tribune*, May 19, 1860.
[68] *Ibid.*, May 25, 1860.

The *Tribune* scorned the accusation that the nomination was an accident and declared that it was a foregone conclusion from the day that Indiana went over to Lincoln. Lincoln's "conservative record, his ability displayed against Douglas and his honesty known to the world formed a happy combination for which the country was looking."[69]

During the campaign that followed the nominating conventions, the *Tribune* published a special edition called the *Press and Tribune Campaign Special*, which was sold at cost to clubs and individuals. Literature bearing on the election was distributed by the *Tribune* over the entire Northwest, usually through the agencies of "Wide Awake" organizations and Republican clubs. Included in the documents printed by the *Tribune* were the following:

I. *Life of Abraham Lincoln.* A thirty-two page pamphlet.
II. *Important Facts for the People: Ten Subjects.*
1. Letter of Bates supporting Lincoln.
2. The Three National Platforms.
3. The Wickliffe (slave code) resolutions with extracts from the Dred Scott Decision from Douglas' "Grand Jury Speech," and from Col. Forney's Addresses.
4. Herschel V. Johnson's Slave Code Record.
5. Squatter Sovereignty and the Slave Trade.
6. What Popular Sovereignty has done—Extracts from Mr. Douglas' Speech in the Senate.
7. Slavery in New Mexico—Serfdom of White Laborers.
8. Slavery in Nebraska—Efforts of the Republicans to abolish it—Successful exertions of the Democrats to retain and preserve it.
9. Votes cast for Douglas are practically given to Breckinridge or Old Joe Lane.
10. Lincoln's and Hamlin's letters of acceptance.
III. *Political Record of Stephen A. Douglas on the Slavery Question.* Sixteen pages.

[69] *Chicago Press and Tribune*, June 1, 1860.

IV. *Political Debates Between Hon. Abraham Lincoln and Hon. Stephen A. Douglas.* Two hundred and sixty-eight pages.

V. Speeches by Lincoln, Lovejoy, Wilkinson, Schurz, Sherman and others.[70]

The *Tribune* used its entire resources to put Lincoln before the people. From the day of the nomination to the day when ballots decided the issue, editorials appeared in a steady stream, while the columns of the paper were filled with Republican doctrine. Medill was active in committee work and aided in the efficient management of the campaign in the Northwest. Through his efforts, speakers were placed where they would do the most good and money distributed in so-called "weak spots."[71] Reporters were dispatched with orders to secure all the Lincoln material available in order that he might be placed before the various classes of people in such a way as to command their votes. It was not as brilliant a campaign as that of 1856, but it was intense and full of party enthusiasm. The Republicans, no longer with their backs to the wall, waged an aggressive battle which would have been dangerous to the Democrats, even in normal times. Through it all, the *Tribune* firm, with its paper, from the days preceding the Chicago Convention until the last ballot was counted and Lincoln was declared the next President of the United States, did its part.[72] Some writers think it was more than that, but in either case, once Lincoln became the *Tribune's* choice for President, he received its wholehearted support. There can be little doubt but that the building up of public opinion and the publicity so valuable to a politician were directly aided by the *Tribune*.

---

[70] *Press and Tribune Campaign Documents* (Library of Congress); see also Broadsides Collection in Library of Congress.

[71] "We would like very much to have Sumner make his speech here before Seward comes. Can't you fix the day a week or so before Oct. 20th? . . . This state is going all right. The last twelve days has been spent in working up Northern Illinois and she responds gloriously." Medill to Washburne, Sept. 9, 1860, Washburne MSS. See also Judd to Trumbull, Oct. 15, 1860, Trumbull MSS.

[72] *Chicago Press and Tribune*, July 19, July 26, 1860.

MRS. LINCOLN AS A WHITE HOUSE HOSTESS

By VIRGINIA KINNAIRD*

The career of Mrs. Abraham Lincoln as the wife of a president of the United States began in the prime of her life. She was a comely matron of forty-three when she assumed the duties of the first lady of the land in March, 1861.

She possessed many qualities desirable for such a position. She could preside graciously over social activities. She was intelligent; possessed the education of a cultured woman; was a good conversationalist; was interested in politics, and had associated with political leaders of Illinois and Kentucky; was extremely ambitious for the advancement of her husband's position, and was confident of his ability to succeed. Her prospects seemed bright then in November, 1860, when it was announced that Abraham Lincoln had won the election. It would be difficult to say just what part she had played in his rise to such fame. Biographers have run the gamut of claims: from maintaining that because of her hot temper and shrewish disposition Lincoln stayed away from home and consequently led an active political life, to believing that "without the influence and inspiration of Mary Todd Lincoln, the world would never have known Abraham Lincoln, for he would never have reached the White House without her."[1]

Undoubtedly Mrs. Lincoln had played some part in her husband's fortunes. She had borne four sons of whom he was extremely proud and who offered him a keen incentive. She had

* Teacher of Social Studies in Central High School, Fort Wayne, Ind.
[1] Honoré Willsie Morrow, *Mary Todd Lincoln, An Appreciation of the Wife of Abraham Lincoln* (New York, 1928), 13.

brought refinement and culture to Lincoln. Her acquaintance with prominent families in Springfield and Lexington must have been of some advantage to him. The pride and confidence she displayed in his ability certainly encouraged him.

If she was ambitious for herself as well as for her husband she must have felt proud of the chance which had come to them. She had lived through some very lean years during their early Springfield days. She had sewed for her family and scrimped along on a meager income. Gradually conditions had improved and their entertaining in their Springfield home had received much favorable comment. Now she was to hold the position of the "first lady of the land." It was a sudden rise, perhaps, but she probably felt herself as well equipped as most presidents' wives—and better than some—to assume the arduous tasks awaiting her.

When Mr. Bartlett, a correspondent of the New York *Evening Post*, was sent to Springfield to find out just who and what these people were who were potential occupants of the White House, he reported of Mrs. Lincoln as follows:

> I had the pleasure . . . of a brief interview with Mrs. Lincoln. . . . Whatever of awkwardness may be ascribed to her husband, there is none of it in her. On the contrary, she is quite a pattern of lady-like courtesy and polish. She converses with freedom and grace, and is thoroughly *au fait* in all the little amenities of society. . . . [She] has received a liberal and refined education, and should she ever reach it, will adorn the White House.[2]

Life must have looked very exciting to this woman who hoped to make a good impression in the new position she would fill as hostess of the White House. Neither man nor woman should be criticized for ambition nor for joy in its accomplishment. But these were difficult times which brought the Lincolns into this position. The comparative comfort of other days was not to be enjoyed by them during their occupancy of the White House.

---

[2] D. W. Bartlett, *The Life and Public Services of Hon. Abraham Lincoln* (authorized ed.; New York, 1860), 147.

Washington in 1861 was not the same sleepy, easygoing southern city which had ushered in previous presidential parties. It
had and was undergoing far-reaching changes. By the time of
the inauguration Washington had become an armed camp. The
inaugural parade, in place of a civilian's demonstration, was like
a military expedition, liable to be attacked at any moment. On
April 2, 1861, Mrs. Lincoln wrote to a friend: "Thousands of
soldiers are guarding us, and if there is safety in numbers we have
every reason, to feel secure. We can only hope for peace!"[3] The
White House itself was filled with these soldiers.

The dislike of the former southern residents of Washington
for the things which Lincoln represented in their minds was expressed by a southern woman, still remaining in Washington, in
a letter to a friend who had gone south:

> You would not know this God-forsaken city, our beautiful
> capital, with all its artistic wealth, desecrated, disgraced with
> Lincoln's low soldiery. . . . There are 30,000 troops here. . . .
> They go about the avenue insulting women and taking prop-
> erty without paying for it. . . . Such are the men waged to
> subjugate us of the South.[4]

Society in Washington also experienced a prodigious change.
For years southern women had controlled Washington society.
They smiled good-naturedly at the awkward and perplexed efforts of women from other sections of the country in their attempts to thread the "ins and outs" of Washington's social
labyrinth. But the winter of 1860-1861 saw the beginning of the
exodus of senators from the official body. All Washington seemed
to change.

With the departure of this group came another army in addition to the army of enlisted soldiers: contractors and speculators
eager to make profits out of the necessities of war.

Many old residents regarded this incursion as a great

---

[3] Carl Sandburg and Paul M. Angle, *Mary Lincoln, Wife and Widow* (New
York, 1932), 203.
[4] Virginia Clay-Clopton, *A Belle of the Fifties* (New York, 1905), 151-52.

indignity. . . . Ladies, gentle and refined, who had been accustomed to ease and luxury at the National Capital, looked upon the overdressed wives and companions of the newly-arrived business men as representing the social conditions existing in the North, and fixed their condemnation accordingly.[5]

The heart of any woman ambitious to take her place as the hostess of the White House might well sink at facing this disruptive world of Washington society. To maintain even a semblance of the customary social life of the White House was impossible. Mrs. Lincoln was probably the equal of any of this Washington aristocracy in intelligence, education, culture, and family antecedents, but she was married to a representative of the West, a Republican whose social background did not fit him to assume the social duties of the White House.

Regardless of how zealous the efforts of Mrs. Lincoln might be or how well-fitted she was, her task from the outset was most disheartening. The Washington aristocracy condemned without waiting for proof, and Mrs. Lincoln became the target for criticism. By degrees the Maryland and Virginia families who held sway ceased to appear at formal receptions. They resented the new element of which they considered the Lincolns the embodiment.

As for the new element, exquisite finesse was necessary to draw into harmony these incongruous newcomers. Many forces and divisions within political parties had to be conciliated. Unfortunately Mrs. Lincoln possessed the untoward faculty of forming deep-seated prejudices.

To maintain the customary entertaining expected of White House occupants in the face of these war scares, preparations, and preconceived impressions, was a problem. But Mrs. Lincoln tackled it with good intentions.

Her first appearance before Washington society at large was at the inaugural ball. The *New York World* reported that the

---

[5] *Washington During War Time, A Series of Papers Showing the Military, Political, and Social Phases During 1861 to 1865*, edited by Marcus Benjamin (Washington, D. C., [1902]), 189-90.

guests began to assemble at nine. By ten, between two and three thousand persons were assembled. The President and his party appeared about eleven. Mrs. Lincoln, escorted by Senator Douglas, "was superbly dressed in a blue silk trimmed with Alencon lace and a blue ostrich feather in her hair which was exceedingly becoming."[6] Mrs. Ellett, who was a contemporary of the times, although she does not say whether she herself was present, wrote enthusiastically of Mrs. Lincoln's appearance: "All eyes were turned on Mrs. Lincoln, whose exquisite toilet and admirable ease and grace, won compliments from thousands." An eyewitness said, "Mrs. Lincoln, always amiable and dignified, was tonight more charming than ever."[7]

The social amenities of the White House had consisted of state dinners and receptions; the former dedicated to the entertainment principally of foreign ministers and heads of departments; the latter to "the people" in the widest acceptance of the term. During the few weeks following the inauguration, Mrs. Lincoln began to hold receptions each Saturday afternoon when the conservatory on the west terrace was thrown open to callers. By this means she evidently intended to draw the support of influential persons who would aid the administration. W. H. Russell, the correspondent of the *London Times*, received an invitation with a magnificent bouquet of flowers; a card was attached with Mrs. Lincoln's compliments and another card announcing a reception at three o'clock. He arrived rather late and there were only two or three ladies in the drawing room. He was informed afterwards that the attendance had been "very scanty." His comment in his diary was: "The Washington ladies have not made up their minds that Mrs. Lincoln is the fashion. They miss their Southern friends, and constantly draw comparisons between them and the vulgar Yankee men and women who are now n power."[8]

---

[6] *New York World*, March 5, 1861.

[7] Mrs. E. F. Ellett, *The Court Circles of the Republic* (Hartford, Conn., 1869), 534.

[8] William Howard Russell, *My Diary, North and South* (Boston, 1863), 53-54.

Mrs. Lincoln essayed her first state dinner on March 28, 1861. Elizabeth Todd Grimsley, a cousin of Mrs. Lincoln's and a guest at the White House at this time, wrote that this dinner was not a gay affair as few ladies of the Cabinet members were in Washington. Seward's daughter-in-law acted in place of his wife and Bates was represented by his daughter, Mrs. Bates being a domestic woman.

When it came to the first public reception there arose an argument because Seward as Secretary of State wished to give the first official entertainment, while Mrs. Lincoln objected, urging that the first official entertainment should be given by the President. The same endeavor that Seward showed in his relation to government affairs with the President is shown here in this small matter, his desire to take precedence. Lincoln's letter in reply to Seward's suggestion that he would be willing to assume the responsibility of adopting a policy and pursuing it remains. Tactfully, but in no uncertain terms, it says, "I remark that if this must be done, I must do it."[9] We have no such remains of what passed between Mrs. Lincoln and Seward. Inasmuch as she was a woman of determination who knew what she wanted and insisted on getting it, we can imagine what the argument was like. Mrs. Ninian Edwards in 1866 wrote that Mrs. Lincoln had an argument with Seward at the time she was in the White House and she heard Mrs. Lincoln say, "I'll show you that my husband is the President."[10]

Here was an unfortunate beginning, for the Secretary of State generally acts as a social guide in diplomatic relations. Undoubtedly Mrs. Lincoln meant to protect her husband's interests but in so doing she had developed a mutual prejudice. Mrs. Lincoln won the argument and the first reception was held on April 8.

This at least was well attended. It was a monstrous gathering. The oldest frequenters of White House receptions declared they

---

[9] Letter to Seward, April 1, 1861, *Complete Works of Abraham Lincoln*, edited by John G. Nicolay and John Hay (Gettysburg ed.; New York, 1905), VI: 237.

[10] Letter written to Dr. Barton (in the Lincoln collection of the University of Chicago Library).

had never seen so many people pass through the House at any previous time, nor was it ever excelled in brilliancy. An hour before the doors were opened, the great driveway was blocked with carriages and the sidewalks and approaches to the White House were thronged with ladies and gentlemen waiting to pay their respects to the President and Mrs. Lincoln. By half past eight the crowd was so dense inside and so great outside that it was necessary to pass ladies and gentlemen who wished to leave out the windows. This mode of exit lasted for an hour.

Charles Francis Adams gives an account of his experiences there:

> A pretty business it was. Such a crush was, I imagine, never seen in the White House before on a similar or any other occasion. . . . It was a motley crowd. There they were— the sovereigns; some in evening dress, others in morning suits, with gloves and without gloves, clean and dirty, all pressing in the same direction and all behaving with propriety.[11]

The *National Republican* of Washington D. C. reported during the year that these various receptions open to the public were largely attended, particularly by the military people who came to the city. On August 1, 1861, an item stated that the President and Lady were both in their usual good spirits, and received their guests with that urbanity and ease for which they were proverbial.

It was during this summer that Prince Napoleon came to America. His visit to Washington was again the source of argument between Mrs. Lincoln and Seward, if Mrs. Grimsley's statement can be relied upon. Seward again suggested that he be the first to give the dinner following the Prince's arrival. Mrs. Lincoln objected and she straightway made plans with Hay and Nicolay, the President's secretaries, for a formal dinner. Seward entertained two evenings later. The *New York World* bore the following account: "Mrs. Lincoln, charmingly dressed, looked so young and blooming, it seemed a good joke for her to introduce

---

[11] *Charles Francis Adams, 1835-1915: An Autobiography* (Boston, 1916), 99-100.

Mrs. Lincoln as a White House Hostess

as her son the youth, a head taller than herself, who accompanied her. She went out to dinner on the Prince's arm."[12]

The state dinners during the early years of the war became very difficult to continue. Mrs. Lincoln felt that they were expensive and therefore should be abolished or lessened in number during the war. Furthermore, there was always the constant fear that some official entertainment would be disrupted by the arrival of bad news from the front. So they tried to crowd many affairs into one and gave a ball which was a reception with refreshments, with no room afforded for dancing. The official reporters were not given cards as guests and so were angered—always a dangerous situation.[13]

The description of this event in *Leslie's* read:

> The guests arrived by half-past nine and were received by Mr. and Mrs. Lincoln with a gracious welcome and a kind word. The salon, when filled, presented the aspect no doubt contemplated and designed by Mrs. Lincoln of a large, select and elegant private party, with its animated conversational groups relieved by the gay dress of the ladies, and the uniforms of the army. . . . The promenade was led off about eleven by Mr. Lincoln with Miss Browning, daughter of Senator Browning of Illinois, and Mrs. Lincoln with Senator Browning.
>
> The regular supper was set in the dining room and was considered one of the finest displays of the confectioners art ever seen in this country.[14]

In spite of the glowing approval of the ball given in *Leslie's*, such was not the case in other quarters. "Mrs. Lincoln's presuming to abolish the time-honored but costly state-dinner of the White House, increased her personal unpopularity to an intense degree" with some groups.[15] Any attempt to change social customs in the White House always brings criticism. In this democracy the public feels its right to dictate over the national home.

---

[12] *New York World*, Aug. 8, 1861.
[13] William O. Stoddard, *Inside the White House in War Times* (New York, 1890), 194-95.
[14] *Frank Leslie's Illustrated Newspaper*, Feb. 22, 1862.
[15] Mary Clemmer Ames, *Ten Years in Washington* (Hartford, 1882), 172

Criticism of entertainments came from all sides. Some made fun of them and brought forth parodies of sarcasm. One Phila-delphia rhymester wrote such a piece entitled "The Queen Must Dance," while another doggerel was entitled "The Charge of the Light Brigade." Concerning an evening reception at the White House on February 5, 1862, Mrs. Ames said:

> The Abolitionists throughout the country were merciless in their criticisms of President and Mrs. Lincoln for giving this reception when the soldiers of the Union were in cheer-less bivouacs or comfortless hospitals.[16]

To entertain or not to entertain was the problem. Some thought Mrs. Lincoln had no right to change the customs of the White House while some thought she ought to close it to every species of festivity or social observance.

After this famous party there were few brilliant festivities during the war. But Mrs. Lincoln's afternoon receptions and the President's public levees were held regularly during the winters, and the customary New Year's Day reception each year brought crowds of callers to the White House. The evening levees were usually held twice a week during the winter, those on Tuesday evenings being so-called dress receptions and the Saturday levees being less formal in character.[17]

The best sources of information on Mrs. Lincoln's manage-ment in the White House are the employees themselves. Lin-coln's secretaries were liable to be called upon by Mrs. Lincoln to assist her in various capacities. William O. Stoddard, who was one of these when the Lincolns first took over the rule of the White House, wrote his account of his experiences several years later.

> Mrs. Lincoln is absolute mistress of all that part of the White House inside of the vestibule, on the first floor, and of all the upper floor east of the folding doors across the

---

[16] Ben: Perley Poore, *Perley's Reminiscences of Sixty Years in the National Metropolis* (Philadelphia, 1886), II: 120.
[17] Noah Brooks, *Washington in Lincoln's Time* (New York, 1896), 67.

MRS. LINCOLN AS A WHITE HOUSE HOSTESS   73

hall at the head of the stairs. She has had varied assistance in the management of her domain since she came into possession of it. She was never less than a somewhat authoritative ruler of her own affairs, but it is entirely easy . . . to meet her with the most positive and strenuous negatives. She is always ready to listen to argument and to yield to plainly put reasons for doing or for not doing, provided the arguments come from a recognized friend, for her personal antipathies are quick and strong, and at times find hasty and resentful forms of expression.[18]

Stoddard also declared:

Her instructions are given in a very kindly and vivacious manner. As you look at her and talk with her, the fact that she has so many enemies strikes you as one of the moral curiosities of this venomous time, for she has never in any way harmed one of the men and women who are so recklessly assailing her.

There were fewer servants than there had been before. Mrs. Lincoln gave a good deal of personal supervision to the domestic affairs of the White House.[19] She was criticized for this by those who thought a socially correct hostess would not stoop to personal supervision.

One of the first efforts Mrs. Lincoln turned her attention to was the redecoration of the White House.

A visitor at the White House about the time of the exit of Mr. Buchanan would have been struck by the bare, worn, and soiled aspect of that part of the house devoted to the official Executive, an aspect not unlike that presented by "the breaking up of a hard winter" about a deserted farmstead.[20]

The elegance of the mansion had been concentrated on the East, Blue and Red rooms, and the family apartments were in a deplorably shabby condition. An appropriation was made by Congress for refurnishing some of the rooms. Mrs. Lincoln with-

---

[18] Stoddard, *Inside the White House*, 62, 86.
[19] William H. Crook, *Through Five Administrations* (New York, 1910), 17.
[20] Albert G. Riddle, *Recollections of War Times* (New York, 1895), 17.

out a doubt enjoyed the chance of making these improvements.

By November 8, 1861, according to the papers, the White House had undergone a thorough renovation. Some very important improvements had been made, especially in the culinary department, and in the principal rooms which had all been papered and painted. Mrs. Ames, a writer and woman of social prominence in Washington circles, but never a very ardent admirer of Mrs. Lincoln, nevertheless gave her credit for her taste:

> The most exquisite carpet ever on the East Room was a velvet one chosen by Mrs. Lincoln. Its ground was of pale sea green, and in effect it looked as if ocean, in gleaming and transparent waves, were tossing roses at your feet.[21]

Dressing rooms were arranged for ladies upstairs and the conservatory was opened for public levees.

It also fell to Mrs. Lincoln's pleasure to choose a set of china which the White House needed at this time. The set chosen was patriotically designed with an eagle in the center, mounted by clouds, and round the edges was a rim of plain maroon.[22]

Apparently gossip ran rife concerning Mrs. Lincoln's household management. Due to divided opinions of people in Washington, every one of her little foibles, every social *faux pas* she made, has been pounced upon, exaggerated, and held up to public scorn. An item in Charles Francis Adams' diary describing a reception held at Mrs. Eames's a week after the inauguration says:

> All manner of stories were flying about, about Mrs. Lincoln. She wanted to do the right thing, but not knowing how, was too weak and proud to ask; she was going to put the White House on an equal basis, and to that end, was about to dismiss "the help" as she called the servants; some of whom it was asserted had already left because they must live with gentle folks; she had got hold of newspaper reporters and railroad conductors as the best persons to go to for advice and direction.[23]

---

[21] Ames, *Ten Years in Washington*, 171.
[22] Crook, *Through Five Administrations*, 18.
[23] *Autobiography*, 103.

Numberless stories of this sort were current.

W. H. Russell, the correspondent for the *London Times*, made his usual pertinent remarks in his diary toward the end of the year 1861—after he had had a chance to become well acquainted with Washington society:

> The ladies in Washington delight to hear or to invent small scandals connected with the White House; thus it is reported that the Scotch gardener left by Mr. Buchanan has been made a lieutenant in the United States Army, and has been specially detached to do duty at the White House, where he superintends the cooking. Another person connected with the establishment was made Commissioner of Public Buildings, but was dismissed because he would not put down the expense of a certain state dinner to the public account, and charge it under the head of "Improvement to the Grounds." But many more and better tales than these go round, and it is not surprising if a woman is now and then put under close arrest, or sent off to Fort McHenry for too much *esprit* and inventiveness.[24]

To be beautifully dressed was one of the qualifications Mrs. Lincoln thought necessary for her position. The story is told that when it became certain that Lincoln was elected, he and Mrs. Lincoln went to Chicago, where she bought a dress for the inaugural ceremonies. When they returned home and were unpacking their purchases, Mr. Lincoln said: "Well, wife, there is one thing very likely to come out of this scrape, anyhow. We are going to have some new clothes."[25] Whether Lincoln ever said it or not, Mrs. Lincoln got the new clothes. The critical press criticized her for extravagant dressing in war times, but other women suffered the same criticism.

Due to the Jenkinism of the press, Mrs. Lincoln's gowns were meticulously described. They were evidently in very good taste, and her appearance as a White House hostess was pleasing. The article in the *Herald* describing the second inaugural ceremonies

---

[24] Russell, *My Diary*, 567.
[25] *Lincoln's Own Stories*, edited by Anthony Gross (New York, 1912), 70.

is somewhat more conservative in its description than many, and probably gives a fair picture of her appearance.

> Mrs. Lincoln's dress was of black velvet trimmed with ermine. She was dressed with great elegance, and was the center of attraction, not any more from the fact of her being the wife of the President than the fact of the elegance and exceeding good taste of her dress and general queen-like bearing. It will probably be impossible to find more taste displayed by ladies in their costumes than those in the gallery. Mrs. Lincoln was second to none in the group.[26]

Overzealous newspaper correspondents and gossip constantly brought Mrs. Lincoln before the public. Those that praised her so "out-Heroded Herod" that they probably gave as much satisfaction to her enemies as those that condemned her outright. Gossip will ever play havoc with any reputation.

Satisfying the public in filling the position of hostess of the White House would require the acme of perfection in charm, refinement, and good taste. Many of the wives of the presidents are more or less nonentities because of their lack of these graces. Two hostesses who stand out brilliantly in this capacity are Dolly Madison and Harriet Lane. Indeed, succeeding the niece of President Buchanan as hostess in the White House might be considered one of Mrs. Lincoln's handicaps. This young attractive woman was known as the "toast of two continents," having been received with enthusiasm in England by Queen Victoria and her court, and having filled most creditably her position in the White House.

But how did Mrs. Lincoln impress people who saw her presiding over social affairs, and who had no personal prejudices favoring or opposing her? The following impressions are from memoirs of people who came to call or be received at receptions. Senator Cole from California explained that at the White House soirees the guests were expected to pay their respects first to the President and the members of his family, after which general

---

[26] *New York Herald*, March 6, 1865.

greetings and conversation ensued. "Mr. Lincoln was remarkably genial and agreeable on these occasions and his good wife was not much behind him in this regard."[27]

Senator Harlan of Iowa, whose daughter married Robert Lincoln, has described Mrs. Lincoln:

> She was fair, of about medium height, but standing near her husband, by comparison seemed short. Her quiet, gentle manners and firm womanly bearing impressed everyone with the conviction that she was a well-educated, cultured lady, accustomed to the usages of society and with ability to take care of herself.[28]

In a letter to his wife, Senator Washburne of Illinois wrote that Madame was very gracious when he saw her.[29]

Her ability to put people at their ease is evidenced in the story Howard tells of his experience at a semi-private reception when he was a young man acting as a secretary to his father, then senator from Michigan. He felt the proper thing to do when he was introduced to Mrs. Lincoln was to have a little impromptu conversation with her. He remarked that he understood her son Robert was present and he hoped to have the pleasure of meeting him. She quickly replied that she would take his arm and they would look for him. At first in confusion at this honor of attention bestowed upon him by the first lady, he offered his left arm. Mrs. Lincoln said, "Your other arm, if you please," and as they started off made some playful remark about "we westerners."[30]

General Meade wrote to his wife on April 11, 1863:

> Since our review [by the President and his party] I have attended other reviews and have been making myself (or at least trying so to do) very agreeable to Mrs. Lincoln, who

---

[27] Cornelius Cole, *Memoirs of Cornelius Cole* (New York, 1908), 195-96.

[28] Katherine Helm, *The True Story of Mary, Wife of Lincoln* (New York, 1928), 167.

[29] Letter to Mrs. Washburne, May 17, 1862, in Gaillard Hunt, *Israel, Elihu and Cadwallader Washburn* (New York, 1925), 203.

[30] Hamilton Gay Howard, *Civil War Echoes; Character Sketches and State Secrets*, 73.

seems an amiable sort of personage.[31]

It is human nature to view people in the light of your own interests. Jane Swisshelm was an ardent abolitionist, and during the war years she was well known as a lecturer and newspaper writer of note. She came to Washington strongly prejudiced against Mrs. Lincoln because of her southern birth which she felt would make her a slave sympathizer. She refused to see her and let four public receptions go by without attending. Finally she was prevailed upon to attend the levee of March 2, 1863. When Mrs. Lincoln was pointed out she was much surprised for she appeared so different from what she had expected. Her description in her letter of March 18 was as follows:

> Her complexion is fair as that of a young girl, her cheeks soft, plump and blooming, and her expression tender and kindly. . . . The dress was something that looked elegant and appropriate—nothing incongruous, nothing tawdry. . . . Her hair . . . is abundant, dark and glossy. . . . She stood receiving her guests with quite as much grace and more dignity than I had seen [in] the celebrated Betty Bliss [Mrs. Silas S. Bliss, daughter of Zachary Taylor] when in the same position.[32]

Two foreign correspondents have given us pictures of their impressions of this first lady. The following is from Russell's *Diary* of March 18, 1861.

> Mrs. Lincoln was already seated to receive her guests. . . . Her manners and appearance [are] homely, stiffened, however, by the consciousness that her position requires her to be something more than plain Mrs. Lincoln, the wife of the Illinois lawyer; she is profuse in the introduction of the word "sir" in every sentence, which is now almost an Americanism confined to certain classes, although it was once as common in England. Her dress I shall not attempt to describe, though it was very gorgeous and highly colored. She handled a fan with much energy, displaying a round, well-proportioned

---

[31] *The Life and Letters of George Gordon Meade*, edited by George Meade (New York, 1913), I: 364.
[32] *Crusader and Feminist, Letters of Jane Grey Swisshelm*, edited by Arthur J. Larsen (St. Paul, Minn., 1934), 189.

arm, and was adorned with some simple jewelry. Mrs.
Lincoln struck me as being desirous of making herself agreeable; and I own I was agreeably disappointed, as the Seces-
sionist ladies at Washington had been amusing themselves
by anecdotes which could scarcely have been founded on
fact.[33]

M. Laugel, a French visitor, called with his wife upon Mrs.
Lincoln in January, 1865. He recorded in his diary that Mrs.
Lincoln's language occasionally indicated her humble background,
but that she was very discreet. He said that though General
Butler was severely criticized, Mrs. Lincoln was very diplomatic.

> She spoke becomingly of an old female friend now a flam-
> ing secessionist. Of the soldiers she spoke, quite unconscious-
> ly, as a Princess might have done: "In our public ceremonies,
> what I always like to see best is our dear blue-coats."[34]

The Washington correspondent for the *New York Times* described her in the receiving line as exhibiting an unexpected self-
possession.

> Had she been born and bred in Washington, accustomed
> from childhood to surroundings of most prominent position,
> she could not have exhibited less anxiety, less embarrassment
> or more "savoir faire."[35]

The writer accredited her with three valuable characteristics
"common sense, self confidence, and tact," and speaks of her as
possessing a "pleasing manner, open heart, and a working brain."
From this cross section of guests at the White House the conclusion may be drawn that Mrs. Lincoln appeared to good advantage as a White House hostess. She had the ability to make people
feel at ease when she wished to do so. She had an inherent hospitality and an interest in people which served her to good advantage.

---

[33] Russell, *My Diary*, 41-42.
[34] Auguste Laugel, "A Frenchman's Diary in our Civil-War Time," *The Nation*, July 31, 1902, p. 89.
[35] *Lexington Observer and Reporter*, March 23, 1861, quoting the *New York
Times*.

The charges of her sympathizing with the rebel cause probably gave rise to the criticisms that she did not do her share in aiding the war work of the women. Numerous witnesses, however, give evidence that Mrs. Lincoln did her part in visiting hospitals and bringing comfort and pleasure to the wounded soldiers.

Mrs. Ann S. Stephens, the distinguished novelist, often accompanied her on these visits of mercy, and described the scene as most interesting—to see the wife of the President walking for hours through the wards to say cheering words of hope and encouragement to the wounded and sick; laying fresh flowers on their pillows, and offering them delicacies brought from the White House. Her carriage would be laden with flowers and baskets of dainties, fruits, &c., for these hapless ones.[36]

A letter, written by Mrs. Annie M. Allen from Washington, D. C., December 25, 1862, to Mrs. J. A. Logan, says:

Mrs. Lincoln and Mrs. Caleb B. Smith have made grand preparations for Christmas dinners in different hospitals.[37]

Of these same preparations the *New York Herald* said:

Mrs. Lincoln received on Monday the large quantity of turkeys, chickens, etc. purchased for her in Chester County, Pennsylvania to be donated to the hospitals here for Christmas dinner. The superintendents of each hospital are invited to present themselves tomorrow and the next day at the Executive Mansion and receive an ample quota for the benefit of their patients.[38]

Among the dispatches sent by Lincoln is one to Hiram Barney in New York which says:

Mrs. L. has $1,000 for the benefit of the hospitals and she will be obliged, and send the pay if you will be so good as to select and send her $200 worth of good lemons and $100

---

[36] Ellett, *Court Circles of the Republic*, 526.
[37] Letter in the Logan Papers of the Library of Congress. (Mrs. Allen was probably the wife of Representative William J. Allen from Illinois).
[38] *New York Herald*, Dec. 24, 1862.

worth of good oranges.[39]

The *New York Tribune* quoted the *Washington Republican* as follows:

> It may not be known that Mrs. Lincoln has contributed more than any lady at Washington, from her private purse, to alleviate the sufferings of our wounded soldiers; and it is but just to add that day by day her carriage is seen in front of the hospitals, where she distributes with her own hands delicacies prepared in the kitchen of the White House.[40]

Stoddard said that Mrs. Lincoln often visited hospitals. He added:

> She rarely takes outside company with her upon these errands, and she thereby loses opportunities. If she were wordly wise she would carry newspaper correspondents, from two to five, of both sexes, every time she went, and she would have them take shorthand notes of what she says to the sick soldiers and of what the sick soldiers say to her. Then she would bring the writers back to the White House and give them some cake and ... coffee. By keeping up such a process she could somewhat sweeten the contents of many journals. ... The directly opposite course, as she pursues it, has not by any means worked well.[41]

Mrs. Lincoln's "working brain" showed an active interest in the progress of the war. She apparently enjoyed visiting navy yards and army camps, to be shown the preparations and maneuvers. The newspapers of the time frequently related accounts of such expeditions. As the President's wife, she was given great acclaim by the soldiers.

Mrs. Lincoln occasionally accompanied the President to headquarters at the front. One such visit occurred about the middle of July, 1864, at the time Early's dash upon Washington was causing a good deal of panic in the country in general. The news

---

[39] Dispatch of Aug. 16, 1862, Nicolay and Hay, *Complete Works of Abraham Lincoln*, VIII: 10-11.
[40] *New York Tribune*, Jan. 29, 1863.
[41] Stoddard, *Inside the White House*, 87-88.

of the approach of Early was brought to the city by the panic-stricken people from the Maryland villages near by who came flocking into Washington, flying in wild disorder, and bringing their household goods with them. The city was cut off at the north and east. For two or three days there were no telegraphic messages, no mail, and no railway travel. Washington was in a ferment, men were marching to and fro; able-bodied citizens were swept up and put into the District Militia. Washington stood agape listening to the sound of the rebel cannon less than ten miles away. The Lincoln family was at its summer residence, the Soldiers' Home, on the outskirts of the city, about halfway between the outer line of fortifications at Fort Stevens and the city.

Mr. and Mrs. Lincoln went to Fort Stevens during the skirmish and faced the fire of the rebel forces. People blamed various persons for the defenseless conditions of the capital—General Halleck, General Augur, the Secretary of War, and the President. Because of the failure of the Union forces to follow the attack of the rebel forces, they retreated to Richmond unharmed. Mrs. Lincoln laid the failure to Stanton. Later, when Stanton was calling on the Lincolns, he said to Mrs. Lincoln: "I intend to have a full-length portrait of you painted, standing on the ramparts at Fort Stevens overlooking the fight."

Mrs. Lincoln with her caustic wit replied: "That is very well, and I can assure you of one thing, Mr. Secretary, if I had had a few *ladies* with me the Rebels would not have been permitted to get away as they did."[42]

Undoubtedly, Mrs. Lincoln enjoyed "playing politics" which, to many people, was one of her irritating traits. Politicians often accused her of dabbling in affairs where, according to their opinions, she did not belong.

When one considers the conditions existing in regard to appointments to office due to the war, it is not surprising that a President's wife should be besieged by office seekers, and considering her interest in what was going on, it is no wonder that she

[42] F. B. Carpenter, *Six Months at the White House* (New York, 1866), 301-302.

had a share in helping to fill them.   In her interest in politics she
was a bit in advance of her times, perhaps.   In the light of the
present day such activity on the part of a President's wife can
be viewed with more understanding and less unfavorable comment.

There were hundreds of new positions to be filled and thousands of office seekers desiring to fill them.   Anyone having any
influence or related in any way to anyone with influence was besieged.   Even Tad Lincoln was besought to use his influence.

Before Mrs. Lincoln left Springfield she began to urge or discourage certain appointments that were being considered.   Among
the papers of Judge David Davis is a letter written by her, urging
Davis to discourage the appointment of Judd to a cabinet position.[43]

Secretary Bates wrote in his diary on February 2, 1862:

There is a formidable clique organized against Mr. Seward,
who, fearing his adroitness, work very privily against him.
Their object (at least *friend* Newton thinks so) is to compel
his retirement and put senator Harris in his place.   It is said
that some of them have approached Mrs. Lincoln and not
without success, making her believe that Mr. Seward is laboring with persistent effort, to override the Prest. and make
himself the chief man of the adm[inistratio]n.   They do tell
me that she is made fully to believe *that*, but I have not seen
any action of hers, in consequence.[44]

A letter which may have aided in giving rise to the stories
later told about gifts bestowed for contracts received is one
written by her to Colonel John Scott.   It reads: "A friend of
mine, has written to me from Kentucky, that he himself has,
from 500 to 1,000 of the finest young Ky. horses.   He is a good
Union man & wishes to dispose of them to the Government, at
Gov. prices."   Mrs. Lincoln goes on to explain that she would
be very much obliged if he could favor her by giving authority

[43] Harry E. Pratt, "David Davis, 1815-1886," *Transactions of the Illinois State
Historical Society for the Year 1930* (Springfield, 1930), 168.
[44] *The Diary of Edward Bates, 1859-1866*, edited by Howard K. Beale (*Annual
Report of the American Historical Association*, IV, Washington, D. C., 1933),
227-28.

to Major Belger, the quartermaster, "to buy these horses at government prices, subject to government inspection." Her reasons for this desire were her pride in Kentucky and the pleasure she would derive from having the horses used in a battle for the Union.[45] Mrs. Lincoln was probably sincere in this letter. She enjoyed doing favors for her friends and here was a chance to express her loyalty to the Union, and her pride in Kentucky; but in a day when bribery in matters of government contracts was rife, it was easy for people to draw unjust conclusions.

The prejudices Mrs. Lincoln developed toward certain persons may have caused her to lose some chances of helping her husband by cultivating friendships which might have been advantageous. But when she had no reason for prejudice, she was very anxious to make such contacts. Her cultivation of Sumner's friendship proved of value to Lincoln, and while it may have been established for reasons of political expediency it probably was not a difficult task for her. A very cordial relationship was established. Mrs. Lincoln showed him many acts of friendship, sometimes in flowers sent to his lodgings and in invitations to meet other guests informally at the White House. She frequently exchanged books with him, and discussed pending questions. Sumner's biographer said: "Her notes to Sumner betoken a lady, kindly, refined, and of intellectual tastes."[46]

At the time of the second inauguration the difference of opinion between Lincoln and Sumner over reconstruction plans had been so radical and outspoken that an actual rupture of their personal relations was currently reported and widely believed. In spite of their disagreements each esteemed the other highly. When Lincoln heard of this rumor regarding their personal rupture, he resolved to discredit it by an open demonstration. On the day of the inaugural ball, Sumner received a note from Lincoln himself requesting him to go as their guest and stating that their carriage would call for him. Upon arriving at the ballroom, the

---

[45] Sandburg and Angle, *Mary Lincoln*, 210-11.
[46] *Memoirs and Letters of Charles Sumner*, edited by Edward L. Pierce (London, 1893), 231.

President asked Sumner to escort Mrs. Lincoln into the room. The Senator thus appeared as one of Lincoln's dearest and most honored friends. This ended the talk of a personal rupture.

Could Mrs. Lincoln have foreseen the tragedy that was to exist for her in the White House, how different might her ambitions for her husband have been. No other presidential family ever suffered such sorrowing years. The sadness of war times marred the pleasure of the honor usually accruing to the first family of the land. But when sorrows came to the Lincolns they came "not single spies but in battalions." Intense personal grief fell upon them in February, 1862, when their third son, Willie, died.

Mrs. Lincoln was completely crushed. She was criticized for showing her grief; her critics claimed that she was selfish in considering her own sorrow at a time when the nation of mothers was undergoing like suffering. Some of the White House entertaining was omitted for a time. Among these the thing which annoyed the public at large was the interruption for a time of the Marine Band concerts held in the public grounds south of the White House. These concerts were weekly occurrences to which all Washington and all its visitors thronged. These had been stopped by government order at the first threat of war, but when public objection was made they were resumed within a few months. After Willie's death, Mrs. Lincoln objected to their continuance. There was grumbling and discontent because the public felt they were being denied the privilege for private reasons.

After this blow, Mrs. Lincoln began to attend spiritualistic seances from which she seemed to derive some comfort. Revivals of spiritualism are apt to come in war times. Newspapers gave some space to spiritualism, awarding the subject a respectful hearing. That this interest in spiritualism was due merely to the emotions of the times and was an attempt to alleviate her personal sorrow is evident in the fact that she remained a member of the faith in which she had been reared. Mrs. Helm speaks of her as being a dyed-in-the-wool Presbyterian. Dr. Louis A. Warren declares: "The pew occupied by the Lincolns in the New York

Avenue Presbyterian Church has become a memorial to the religious inclinations of the Lincoln family."[47]

In addition to all these difficulties with which Mrs. Lincoln had to contend, she had very poor health. There are letters and notes written canceling engagements which had been arranged, because of her indisposition.

When the time came for the question of Lincoln's renomination, it can well be imagined that both the Lincolns felt they had had enough of this "honor" and glory for which they had once been ambitious.

Certain it is that Mrs. Lincoln had every reason to feel that her exit from Washington would be a relief. That she felt keenly the enmity of Washington is clear if the Marquis de Chambrun understood her correctly. On the way home from a visit to City Point early in April, 1865, the Lincolns were driving in the carriage with the Marquis. He gave the following account:

> We were nearing Washington when Mrs. Lincoln, who had hitherto remained silently looking at the town a short distance off, said to me: "That city is filled with our enemies." On hearing this the President raised his arm and somewhat impatiently retorted, "Enemies! We must never speak of that."[48]

Reflectively spoken, it undoubtedly reveals the true expression of her feelings, and well might she feel so. "High-bred, proud, brilliant, witty, and with a will that bent everyone else to her purpose,"[49] she had indeed suffered the breaking of that will.

Her every move seemed to call down from some source censure or even stronger accusation and condemnation. Her husband shared the same constant fire of criticism and when she read aloud the newspaper charges made against him, he would say "Don't do that, for I have enough to bear, yet I care nothing for them.

---

[47] *Lincoln Lore* (*Bulletin of the Lincoln National Life Foundation*), No. 317, May 6, 1935.

[48] Marquis de Chambrun, "Personal Recollections of Mr. Lincoln," *Scribner's Magazine*, Vol. XIII, no. 1 (Jan., 1893), 35.

[49] W. H. Lamon, *The Life of Abraham Lincoln* (Boston, 1872), 238.

If I'm right I'll live, if I am wrong I'll die anyhow, so let them pass unnoticed." Then she would playfully say, "That's the way to learn, read both sides."[50] Could she but as playfully have forgotten the criticisms leveled against her!

When one becomes a servant of the public, he faces a constant firing squad. No act is performed, no move is made, no thought is conceived that does not suffer the criticism of the individuals who create public opinion. Such a servant should possess an ironclad mental attitude in order that the shells may glance off leaving the victim unharmed. Lincoln died a martyr to the cause of "Union." In the policies he pursued in his public services as President of the United States, he won such acclaim that all his faults and personal eccentricities have either become submerged or enshrouded in a halo of glory. A President's wife, lacking the chance of obtaining such a protective covering of fame, needs must be a paragon of all virtues. Mary Todd Lincoln was not one, and, indeed few there are, but no one lacks some virtues, and Mrs. Abraham Lincoln had many to commend her.

---

[50] "An Account of What Mrs. Lincoln Told Me in 1866" (Memorandum from Herndon MS in the collection of Oliver Barrett, Chicago).

MUSEUM PROJECTS IN ILLINOIS HISTORY
FOR HIGH SCHOOL STUDENTS

By LOUISE A. LANGE*

It has been customary in our American History classes at Bloomington High School to require the students each semester to undertake some project outside of their regular class work. These have taken the form of reading historical novels or biographies, of writing papers on assigned topics, or perhaps, very occasionally, projects of the handicraft type. Several years ago, in casting about for some new form of study for my classes, the possibility of using the McLean County Historical Society museum occurred to me. I found the custodians most willing to co-operate in the matter, and thus a new type of project was launched.

The major idea in these undertakings is for the student to choose some item of local history which appeals to him, read about it in books, newspapers, and manuscripts available in the museum, supplement this information, if he chooses, with interviews, examination of relics, etc., and write up his findings in a paper, which, if well done, is made a part of our files on local history.

These projects serve four major purposes, the first and most obvious of which is to acquaint students with local history and people. There is no formal place in our course of study for local history. There are a few third grade teachers who use a unit of local history which, a number of years ago, was a regular part of the work of that grade. Any work done in the grade schools now is entirely dependent upon the initiative of the teacher, although a curriculum revision which will make a place for state history is

---

* Teacher of American History and Civics in the High School at Bloomington, Ill.

expected within the next few years. In the high school there are no courses in state or local history. However, the museum projects provide an extremely elastic method of introducing as much or as little local history as time will permit, at whatever point in the course it fits best.

Closely connected with the first purpose is the second: to show the part Bloomington has played in state and national history. Many topics are purely local in scope, of course, but no student who investigates the life of David Davis or Adlai Stevenson can long keep his subject out of national affairs, nor can he keep the late Governor Fifer out of Illinois affairs. Such biographies bring to the student a realization that Bloomington and Bloomingtonians have played a part in making history; that it has not all been done by people "long ago and far away."

Our textbook emphasizes social and economic history, especially in the latter part of the book where there are chapters on the development of transportation, the history of labor in the United States, immigration problems, the development of society and culture, and so on. This gives us an opportunity to correlate many items of local interest with the larger national picture. For instance, if we are studying writers we can turn to McLean County's contribution in Elbert Hubbard or Rachel Crothers. If we are studying the growth of education we might talk about the development of our own public school system, or the history of Illinois State Normal University or Illinois Wesleyan University. When our attention is focused on transportation, we might find a paper on the history of stagecoaches in this part of the country, one on Bloomington's street car system, or an account of the building of the first experimental Pullman car in Bloomington. For events of a more political nature we could turn to the influence of Bloomington men in nominating Lincoln for the presidency, or Lincoln's part in the Anti-Nebraska convention from which came the famous "Lost Speech." Our author mentions David Davis in connection with the Hayes-Tilden election. This usually has no particular significance to the students until they are encouraged to think about local history. In connection with the World War we might use an account of Bloomington's armistice celebration, the experiences of some Bloomingtonians in the war, or perhaps an account of McLean County's efforts to raise money and collect supplies for war purposes.

These projects, of course, force the students to visit the museum, the existence of which was hitherto entirely unknown to many. Contact with old newspapers, relics, etc. in the museum usually stimulates an interest in such historical materials elsewhere.

The fourth purpose of the projects is to give the students some practice in the use of source materials, and some conception as to how historical materials are compiled. Until they have tried writing some history for themselves, they seem never to have thought about how history gets into books.

The proper presentation of the plan to the class is extremely important. We usually engage in an introductory discussion first, about when and where history is made, in order to bring out the fact that history may be local, that the local communities contribute the people and events which are important in the larger areas of history, and that history is being made all the time. To emphasize these points, pupils are asked for examples of Bloomington people or events of importance, either locally or on a broader scale. The second phase of the introductory discussion is about how history is written, introducing the ideas of written and unwritten sources of information, and a few points about evaluating sources. Then the plan for the projects is explained, and a few papers written by students in former classes may be read by way of example of what is expected. The requirements include turning in a paper from 1,500 to 2,000 words in length, with a bibliography. No attempt is made to introduce the use of footnotes.

Originality is encouraged. Interviews have been a very valuable experience for the students. One girl who was writing on Madame Salzman Stevens, a famous singer from Bloomington, first interviewed a sister of the singer and then wrote a letter to Madame Stevens, who is living in Milan, Italy. In due time a lengthy reply came, to the great joy and delight of all the students. Another girl who chose as her subject "Pioneer Doctors" read all she could find on the subject and then wrote her own account of a typical day of a pioneer doctor. It isn't a scholarly treatise, but it has real feeling for the experiences and services of a pioneer doctor. Another student whose history is bad and whose geography is worse, but who has a real talent for art and drama, wrote on the "Passion Play," arranging her theme on paper cut in the form of a cross. She was just as proud of her contribution as any historian might be of a lengthy thesis.

Assignment of topics is done individually, with due consideration of the interests and ability of the pupil, and of the amount and type of material available. A boy working on the business staff of our school newspaper was interested in studying the changes in advertising and general make-up of newspapers as evidenced by the *Daily Pantagraph*. The sheriff's daughter wrote on the history of jails in McLean County. We have found that some of the slower pupils cannot manage to collect many small bits of information and put them together well, so they are guided into topics where most of the material is to be found in one or two articles. The topics involving much gathering of material are suggested to the better students who have the ability to do a more painstaking piece of work. There is a wide variety of topics, including biographies of numerous Bloomington people in all walks of life, histories of various businesses of Bloomington, subjects such as the Blackhawk War, the campaign of 1840 in central Illinois, Indian lore, pioneer experiences, railroad development, and so on.

The pupils work in the museum according to a schedule, signing up for the week they prefer so that they may be distributed over the semester instead of overcrowding the museum near the end of the semester. This schedule is sent to the museum, along with the topics selected, early enough for the custodian to have materials ready for the students. It also makes it possible for us to check their attendance at the museum.

The results of the projects have not been spectacular, but they have been gratifying and well worth the effort. Most evident is a stimulation of pupil interest in local history and source materials. Historical markers, old newspapers from the attic at home, and reminiscent articles in the local newspapers exert an attraction which had previously been lacking. Class work for some becomes much more interesting, especially when it correlates with the individual's project. Moreover, in a few instances, class work improved when there was not any definite relationship between the project topic and the class work. One of our athletes developed quite a lively interest in history when he discovered that he could write on the history of organized baseball in Bloomington. Another boy who wouldn't do his regular class work and who failed to go to the museum when his turn came, finally developed into a reasonably good student when he was corralled and put to work thumbing his way through all the *Pantagraphs* of the World War period to look for items telling how McLean County helped finance the war.

The better papers are kept at school as permanent additions to our files on local history, to be used in the regular class work of future semesters. The historical museum and the public library have made copies of some of them which were especially valuable to them. The library made a bound copy of one long paper giving a history of all the street names of Bloomington. Other papers which have filled a gap in local records are those on local church histories. The fact that the papers are more than just something to be turned in, graded, and forgotten gives the pupils enjoyment and a sense of accomplishment which is decidedly worthwhile. At the end of the first semester in which I tried this plan, I asked the students to write a criticism of it. Many confessed that at first they expected it to be just another task which they weren't going to enjoy, but that they later found they liked it in spite of themselves. One girl said, "I have never had a bigger thrill out of any piece of school work." The main adverse criticism was that there wasn't enough time to use more of the projects in class. Their attitude toward the plan seems to indicate that there would be interest in local history if more of it were offered to them.

Knowledge of local history is, of course, greatly increased. Incidentally, they seem to have an increased appreciation for the work of historians. Typical of this is one boy's remark: "I didn't know it was so hard to write history until I tried it."

TEACHING ILLINOIS HISTORY IN THE TEACHERS' COLLEGES

By RICHARD L. BEYER*

As I understand it, a triple-header is arranged this morning on our general subject, "The Teaching of Illinois History." And if I am not mistaken, my assignment is to discuss this theme from the point of view of an instructor in one of the teachers' colleges of the state.

The teachers' college instructor has a double task with respect to the teaching of Illinois history. In the first place, like the teacher in the public schools, the liberal arts college, and the university, he has the responsibility of illuminating his students concerning the major movements and trends, the outstanding incidents, and the principal characters in our territorial and state history. He tries to inculcate in his students an appreciation of the evolution of Illinois from its pioneer period into its present position as one of the major states in the Union.

But the teachers' college instructor has another responsibility and that is the training of his students so that when they are graduated they will have the knowledge, technique, and equipment to do efficient teaching in the public schools of the state. To use the now hackneyed phrase, this is the handing of the lamp of learning to another generation of teachers. Preparing the teacher of the future obviously means that in the field of Illinois history, as well as in every other subject in the curriculum, the obligation devolves upon the teachers' college to do patient and serious work. It behooves the faculties of the teachers' colleges

* Head of the Department of History at Southern Illinois State Normal University.

to reflect upon this frequently. Slovenly, inadequate work on our part is apt to result in a mediocre crop of teachers for the public schools in Illinois. And this in turn means that generations of grade and high school students will be the victims of a condition traceable directly back to us.

Serving on a teachers' college faculty is always a responsible occupation, but it seems to me that there is a particularly difficult task for us who, from time to time, try to teach Illinois history. The reason is simply this. The students we find in our classes may have had some Illinois history in the rural or city elementary school, but they have had practically none in the high school. We all know that the secondary school curriculum most cordially ignores our state history. This condition was brought home to me with force again just two weeks ago when I made a survey among fifty-two students enrolled at the Southern Illinois Normal University. Of this number, thirty-one had studied Illinois history in the grade school and twenty-one had had none there. Only eight had studied Illinois history in the high school. Moreover, several of the eight indicated that their high school work in the field had come at the fag end of a civics course. In other words this training was probably as brief as it was incidental. This situation naturally means that if the college students have ever learned any state history they have forgotten most of it when they come to us. Hence, the teachers' college instructor must do a tremendous amount of work in building up a background and reviewing in his classes. He cannot take much for granted on the part of the students, and at least in the beginning of the course the work may be so simple, that it might seem absurdly elementary to a classroom visitor. And yet this approach is absolutely necessary before detailed and involved subject matter dare be presented.

I have often felt that Illinois history is the stepchild in the history curriculum of the teachers' colleges. Our students come to us with reasonably good backgrounds in general American history, European, and even ancient history. Here the teacher may assume some prior knowledge, and can build his college class-room work on this foundation. But in Illinois history, assuming the student has had any at all, possibly six years have elapsed since his exposure to the field in the grades, and most of the subject matter is forgotten.

Lest my audience think that I am unfairly belittling the knowledge of the teachers' college undergraduates in Illinois, let me return to my recent investigation at Southern Illinois Normal University. Before I take this up a word of defense for my own college. Our students at Southern are not dullards. Moreover, in general they have had reasonably good teaching in the grades and in the high school. This was disclosed last fall by the results of a social science test given to the freshmen entering at four of the five Illinois teachers' colleges. Our students ranked second—a standing that blasts any erroneous notion that the Egyptians are the victims of sloppy social science teaching in the public schools in the lower end of the state. I have every reason to believe that elsewhere the same conditions that I am about to suggest with respect to Illinois history would obtain. Of fifty-two students investigated, ten of them did not know when Illinois became a state. Here are some of the answers to the query concerning the date of statehood: 1819, 1825, 1848, 1858, 1886, 1888. Two students hadn't the slightest notion. One gave an answer which, like the peace of God, passeth understanding, by suggesting the year 1648. Asked to locate the site of our first state capital, the 52 students gave these replies: Vandalia, 21; Kaskaskia, 15; "Don't know," 9; Springfield, 2; Salem, 2; Shawneetown, 1; Cahokia, 1; and Peoria, 1. Thirty-nine of the 52 could not identify our famous territorial Governor, Ninian Edwards; 46 failed on our first state Governor, Shadrach Bond, while even despite his role in connection with the Missouri Compromise only one of the 52 was familiar with the name of Jesse B. Thomas.

Now I'll confess that these are simple, factual questions—and that is just the point! How is the teachers' college instructor going to discuss causes, results, significance of movements and trends, the inter-relationship of historic forces, the intricacies of our state political, social, and economic life, when even the simplest and most basic of the elementary facts are not a part of our students' intellectual fiber? The students aren't to blame if they are unprepared to do work of college caliber—the fault rests with the training (or lack of it) which has been offered them before they entered a teachers' college, or even a liberal arts college or a university. Frankly, if the institutions of higher learning are to do mature work—work of really college level—two recommendations are to be made: (1) sound basic work for all students in the grades; (2) some further preparation in high school. Without the latter a great gap between the grade school and the college will still exist, and the college will be obliged to continue with ABC lessons instead of an adult approach to the subject.

Students with whom I have talked at Southern Illinois Normal University feel this lack of background keenly, and in general seem to favor the proposition of more work of a preparatory nature on the pre-college level. Says one: "I do not think enough attention is given Illinois history in the grades or high school. Here I am in college, and while I have had five terms of European and American history, yet I do not know one thing about the history of my own state." And another: "I do not believe enough emphasis is placed on Illinois history in the grade and high schools. The largest percentage of the pupils spend the rest of their lives in this state and should know something about Illinois."

As matters stand now with reference to Illinois history, the teachers' colleges seem to be right back where the young Southern Illinois Normal University was in 1874. Robert Allyn, then president of the school, was roundly criticized because of the type of work offered at Carbondale. He refused to inject either profound or spectacular material in the curriculum because he felt that the students were poorly trained in fundamentals. Surveys indicated that the normal school students sixty-four years ago could neither spell nor punctuate; that simple bits of historical and geographic information were not in their possession. Hence, President Allyn contended that before the undergraduates tackled metaphysical abstractions they must get in the normal schools the fundamentals, that should have been provided by the grade and the high schools of southern Illinois. That is the situation with respect to Illinois history in the teachers' colleges today. We must be certain that the students possess some rudimentary background for the subject before we dare lead them into the intricacies and complicated problems in our field.

It is easy to suggest that the high school should do some work in Illinois history, although the effecting of it might not be so simple. History already has an important place in the high school curriculum, and it might be difficult to find space for this additional course. This is particularly true today when other branches of the Social Studies—Economics, Civics, Problems of Democracy, Sociology, Political Science, and yea, even Civilization courses, are hammering at the door. I earnestly refer the problem to those who are framing the new curriculum for the Illinois high schools. Possibly they can devise a solution.

But to turn to the teachers' college again, we find that those who give instruction in Illinois history have other problems facing them. Anyone who has taught the subject is impressed with the vast amount of material with which he must deal. Some of us must feel that more than one course in Illinois history should be given. However, because of limited teaching staffs, the multiplicity of subjects to be taught, the inability of students to enroll for more than one class, it may not be possible to expand the Illinois history beyond one course. To pack all the material into a single course involves careful planning and a thoughtfully outlined program. Without such meticulous arrangement, the teacher will find that the term will be over and he will probably have left our contemporary history untouched. I have the opinion that if our classroom work is to be of the greatest value, the teacher should bring his Illinois history as nearly down to date as possible. I can see no sound argument in favor of neglecting our current Illinois history, and if our subject is worthwhile, as we at this meeting assume it is, we owe a survey of contemporary Illinois to our students.

At the Southern Illinois Normal University we are impressed with the problem of teaching 120 years of state history and generations of pre-state history in one course. Hence, we in the Department of History have made some allocations of the subject matter which seem to be working well. For example, our Illinois history course emphasizes the period from 1818 onward and the instructor need not spend too much time on territorial days. That topic is given full attention in our two courses dealing with the History of the West. The age of exploration in the Illinois Country is reserved for the class in American Colonial History. Moreover, in our classes in the Middle Period and Recent American History we give time to Illinois history. Our Department of English nicely supplements our work with a folklore course, and at the present time our Department of Music, headed by Mr. David S. McIntosh, an authority in the field, is taking an extensive interest in folk songs. Thus in various ways are the students at Southern learning something about the history of their state, and I am hopeful that this approach will gradually counteract the preparation they lack when they come to us from the high school. Certainly our history majors who have had the opportunity to enroll for the various classes that I have mentioned have demonstrated that they have mastered some knowledge and have gained some insight into the history of Illinois.

There is another argument in favor of spreading the history of Illinois into various courses. Not only can more time be covered, but more phases of state history can be introduced. At Southern we definitely try to get away from an overemphasis on political history, and in teaching Illinois history we are interested in economic, social, and intellectual trends. Concerning the latter we have recently given it greater stress than ever before. Our students are prospective teachers and in our college we believe that the teachers in the public schools should know something of the origins and development of education in this state. Hence, the growth of public education is accorded considerable attention. We also try to provide some material on the founding of the colleges, normal schools, and universities in Illinois.

If there are any teachers' colleges, or for that matter liberal arts colleges, which are now neglecting this intellectual history in their History of Illinois classes, we invite them to introduce this work into their course. I am positive that there will be two revelations coming from such a move. First, it will be learned that the ordinary student is entering a new field of study and investigation. I am afraid that at first the undergraduates will exhibit a shockingly limited knowledge of our state's progress in education, and that many of them are quite uninformed about the history of the very institution which they are attending. Secondly, I am sure that these students will reveal a lively interest in the subject. I think that some of the heartiest responses that I have had in my classroom work in some time have come in connection with the introduction of the study of the intellectual history of the state.

Before bringing this paper to a close there is another topic on which I wish to comment. No one knows better than the members of this Society that even though we have made great progress in research and writing in the realm of Illinois history, yet much remains to be done. All of us can name major themes which are still to be exploited. The history of various communities has been neglected. Many of our county histories are antiquated and are in desperate need of revision. The history of mining, journalism, religion, education, and agriculture in the state are all inviting attention. I am appalled to find that no one has written a definitive account of bloody Williamson County with its mine disorders, its Ku Klux Klan dictatorship, its gangland regime. Here is an important, yet lurid subject that should provide the opportunity for fascinating research and the writing of a major historico-economic theme. I have not attempted to do more than mention just a few intriguing avenues of original study and am certain that my brief list can be extensively supplemented by all who are present.

If we are to unearth the facts of Illinois history the business of research cannot be left to the teachers in the universities, liberal arts colleges and teachers' colleges: to the active members of the Illinois State Historical Society: and to a few graduate students and a few dilettantes. The job is one that demands many minds. And here, it seems to me, the state teachers' colleges have an excellent opportunity to assume some leadership.

Annually the Illinois teachers' colleges are turning out several score graduates who have majored in history and who are being placed in the elementary and high schools of the state. I believe that we have a splendid chance in our Illinois history courses to do the following: (1) Point out that there are immense opportunities for research and writing in the field of Illinois history; (2) give the students some training in the technique of historical research; (3) suggest the sources of historical material in Illinois; (4) urge the prospective teachers to enter the field of state history as researchers and writers in order to augment the scholarly productivity in the realm in which we are interested.

If our teachers on the elementary and secondary school levels can be inspired to enter this particular arena of scholarship, I am confident that a greater knowledge of our state will be accorded the world, the individual researcher will be enriched, and his own classroom work should be improved by the introduction of fresh data. I am pleased to be able to say that Southern Illinois Normal University definitely is convincing its graduating seniors that Illinois history is an attractive realm in which to continue their studies, and even happier to observe, in conclusion, that these new teachers have been giving us a heartening response.

TEACHING ILLINOIS HISTORY: THE
UNIVERSITY VIEWPOINT

By RAYMOND PHINEAS STEARNS*

Any consideration or conclusion with reference to the teaching of Illinois history or local history at the University level or any other level of instruction depends, in final analysis, upon both the accepted definition of history and the alleged values or objectives in view in teaching history. As historians and teachers of history agree upon neither of these things, the question becomes exceedingly delicate and complex and tends in the end to be a matter of personal opinion. This is neither the time nor the place to attempt to formulate definitions of history or to set forth values and objectives in teaching it. But a few examples may illustrate the confusion and varying points of view that are almost certain to arise in any discussion of the subject. An historian of a political turn of mind is likely to agree with E. A. Freeman "that history is past politics and that politics are present history."[1] One with an economic bent will treat almost solely of statistical elements in economic production, distribution, and consumption and tend to interpret all human affairs in terms of economic determinism. A philosopher believes that history is "philosophy teaching by examples;"[2] a moralist agrees with Thomas Arnold that "history is a moral lesson,"[3] or writes ecstatically that history "is a voice

---

* Assistant Professor of History, University of Illinois.
[1] E. A. Freeman, *The Methods of Historical Study* (London, 1866), 44.
[2] Henry St. John, Lord Viscount Bolingbroke, *Letters on the Study and Use of History* (London, 1870), "On the Study of History," Letter I, p. 5.
[3] Freeman, *Historical Study*, 6. Arnold's words are different but the idea is the same. See Thomas Arnold, *Introductory Lectures on Modern History*, edited by Henry Reed (New York, 1866); and Arthur Penrhyn Stanley, *The Life and Correspondence of Thomas Arnold* (5th ed., 2 vols., London, 1845), I: 208, 214.

forever sounding across the centuries the laws of right and wrong."[4] A poet might hold with Shelley that history is a "cyclic poem written by time upon the memories of men."[5] One who subscribes heavily to the personal equation in human affairs is likely to see history as Carlyle did when he wrote that "the History of the world . . . was the Biography of Great Men."[6] And finally, the cynic might agree with Napoleon that history is "a fiction previously agreed upon," or even go so far as to accept the statement attributed to Henry Ford that "history is bunk."

Each of these definitions implies specific objectives in the teaching of history which vary as greatly as the definitions themselves. Moreover, only a few of the definitions admit state history or local history of any type to more than passing notice or to an occasional footnote reference. Thus, the political, economic, and moral historians respectively consider history as a valuable handbook for the present and future guidance of statesmen, business forecasters, and watchdogs of public and private morality. These men paint on broad canvasses and seek to establish fundamental laws of form and color. To them state history is only a tiny splotch of pigment skilfully blended into the finished piece with an infinite care for the elements of balance and perspective. The poet and the biographical historian often lack this sense of balance and perspective, but they generally give a larger space to state and local history. The poet and the novelist find as much about human nature in local history as in a broader field and their work has the added literary charm of local color and attractive intimacy. The biographer maintains not only that the biographies of great men taken *in toto* are history in the fullest sense, but also that they serve as interesting and instructive examples for youth and for society at large. Of course, every community has its great men, relatively speaking, and the biographer-historian has an

---

[4] James Anthony Froude, *Short Studies on Great Subjects* (New York, 1868), I: 28.

[5] Quoted in Lucy Maynard Salmon, *Historical Material* (New York, 1933), 3.

[6] Thomas Carlyle, *On Heroes, Hero-Worship, and the Heroic in History* (*The World's Classics*, LXII, London, 1904), Lecture I, p. 14.

almost unlimited field for his endeavors. In a Carlyle's hands the history of Illinois would probably become a series of biographical sketches of notable men from Father Marquette, George Rogers Clark, and Ninian Edwards to Len Small, Pat Nash, and Al Capone. Lastly, the cynic sees no utility in history whatever except, perhaps, its literary and entertainment values. For these purposes, of course, local history is as good as any in the hands of a competent literary medium.

Of course, history is none of these things—and it is all of them. In reality, there are two histories: one which is theoretical and one which is real; one absolute, the other only relative. The first is unwritten and probably it can never be written, for it is history in the abstract or, as Henry Johnson said, "everything that ever happened."[7] The second is written as we know written history, a mere fragment of the sum of past events, selected, arranged, interpreted, and set down by a man or a group of men who, however serious and well-intentioned, have biases and unconsciously formulated opinions from which they cannot free themselves completely. History in this latter sense is the only history we can ever know: we cannot eradicate entirely the subjective element from written history. Accordingly, we hold a multitude of opinions as to its definition, as to its utility, and even as to the specific facts which are to be selected and elevated to the classroom. Upon this basis, then, we may dispute for an unlimited time upon the merits and demerits of teaching Illinois history.

Nevertheless, though we disagree upon all these things, we tend to agree in the main on one point of fundamental educational value which cannot be dissociated from the study of history: the utility of the historical method as applied to problems of human experience. The ability to discover and to treat the raw materials of history with a highly trained critical faculty and to generate airtight conclusions with a minimum of subjectivity—these are the most precious tools of the student of history, far more valuable

---

[7] Henry Johnson, *Teaching of History in Elementary and Secondary Schools* (New York, 1925), 1.

than the content of courses, than the acquisition of multitudinous historical data. For the student can neither know nor remember all the details in history. In training students in the historical method the materials for local history—for Illinois history—are fully as valuable as the materials in the Library of Congress, the British Museum, the Bibliothèque Nationale, or any other great storehouse of historical matter. Indeed, the proximity of the materials gives state history a convenient advantage for such training at all levels of academic instruction.

The Department of History of the University of Illinois is keenly aware of these advantages. Members of the Department have testified to this fact by the preparation of a series of volumes devoted to the history of the state which, taken altogether, comprise the finest state history yet written for any state in the Union. If further testimony is demanded, the library will supply scores upon scores more of bachelors', masters', and doctors' dissertations devoted to various phases of Illinois history. This work is still going on in steady, perhaps increased, volume under the learned direction of Professor T. C. Pease as director of that department in the Graduate School of Arts and Sciences known as the Illinois Historical Survey, an organization "for the purpose of carrying on systematic studies in the history of Illinois."[8] The Illinois Historical Survey is splendidly equipped with a constantly expanding library of source materials in Illinois history and it co-operates with the State Historical Library in the publication of these and other materials in the volumes of the *Illinois Historical Collections*. In the conduct of research in Illinois history the University takes its rightful lead.

A university has a dual responsibility. It is charged with the pioneer task of advancing the intellectual frontiers through original research in all branches of learning; it is also charged with the important task of training youth at collegiate and post-graduate levels through formal course offerings and other types of instruc-

---

[8] *University of Illinois Annual Register, 1936-1937* (Urbana-Champaign, 1937), 293.

tion.   In the first of these responsibilities, as has already been noted, the Department of History of the University of Illinois has carried on and is carrying on its full share of activities as regards the history of the state.   In the second field of endeavor —that of teaching Illinois history—the University is correspondingly active both at the undergraduate and graduate levels of instruction.

For undergraduates, the Department of History offers six courses in American history at different instructional levels and in different periods, in all of which Illinois history figures to a greater or lesser degree.   Further, in any of these courses the student may, if he chooses, prepare term reports and other written papers on local or state historical subjects.   More pertinent still, Professor Pease of the Department of History offers a course entitled the "History of the West" (History 22a-22b) which, though not specifically called a history of Illinois, grew out of a former course with that title and is primarily a history of the Illinois Country; that is, a history of Illinois with necessary and proper perspective designed to show the place of Illinois in the development of the Middle West and of the Nation.   In this course, too, students are given ample opportunity and encouragement to pursue studies in specific topics in Illinois history.   And lastly, among the courses open to undergraduates, there is a "Thesis Course" for honors in history (History 90a-90b), a course designed to give superior history students special training in historical investigation.   A student with a suitable academic record may, with the approbation of the instructor concerned, elect this course in any field of history, which means that he may study Illinois history in any phase approved by his instructor—and approval is not withheld except in instances in which the topic is unsuitable for the proper maintenance of academic standards of work.

In the Graduate School, the Department of History offers similar opportunities to students interested in Illinois history. A series of courses in American history permits special studies in state history; numerous seminars in American history offer even greater opportunities along this same line; a course in research in special topics intended to furnish advice and direction in research and in writing theses is offered by every member of the graduate teaching staff in the Department of History; with the approval of the instructor and of the graduate faculty, a student is free to select topics in Illinois history, and the entire resources of the Illinois Historical Survey's collections of materials are at his disposal. Finally, a course on "The Westward Movement" (History 122a,-b, -c, and -d) is offered by Professor Pease. Similar to the "History of the West" offered for undergraduates, this course offers to students of the graduate school intensive materials on the history of Illinois placed in the broad setting of frontier development and with that perspective and interpretation necessary for the proper historical treatment of the history of the state.

With such an extensive number of courses treating Illinois history directly or indirectly, the University has seen little need for an additional course labeled specifically "The History of Illinois." The pressure of thousands of students, the responsibility for the entire field of history, an already overcrowded curriculum, a teaching staff constantly taxed to its utmost, and financial support inadequate for the needs of the Department—all these are very material and practical reasons why a course in Illinois history as such is not offered. However, the Department is aware of an increasing demand for such a course. There is an increasing interest in state history among the people of this state and of neighboring states. Some state universities are offering courses in state history, and a few states require it in their public school systems. A well-known publishing house, with its commercial ear to the ground, has already started publication of a series of state histories in anticipation of the growing interest and demand. Members of families prominent in the development of Illinois have expressed a desire that a specific course in Illinois history be given at the University. Furthermore, last autumn, a number of students of the University presented a petition which demanded that a course in Illinois history be offered at the University. This petition was drawn by members of an undergraduate organization, the Illini History Club, and was signed by a considerable number of history majors and other undergraduates. Soon after the petition had been presented to the Department of History a committee of the Department was appointed to consider the demand and to investigate the possibilities of offering such a course. Unfortunately, however, because of the illness of members of this committee and the recent death of one of them, Professor Marcus L. Hansen, no formal report has been possible to date. The question will be given due consideration. If the demand is sufficiently active to warrant it and if the financial resources of the Department are enlarged sufficiently to make it possible, a course specifically treating of the history of Illinois will probably be added to the University's curriculum.

The University welcomes the demand for state history as an indication of the cultural and social maturity of the people of the state. But a few warnings are in order as regards the trend of such a movement and its possible consequence in the future. Severe and not wholly undeserved criticism is frequently directed at the curricula of schools and colleges for their increasing specialization—some critics say overspecialization. In history, in particular, one of the major problems of teaching is that of historical synthesis, the attempt to make vital and to give meaning to the great mass of details in history. At all levels of instruction, one means now being employed increasingly in an effort to achieve greater synthesis of materials and to make history more meaningful to students is the preparation of broader and broader survey courses, such as the history of civilization from the amoeba to Hitler, and the even broader synthesis of all the social sciences in one course. A movement towards state history is in many respects a movement that runs counter to this trend in the teaching of history—whether wisely or unwisely it is impossible to say at this point. At best the introduction of courses in state history crowds, even further, curricula which, in many instances, are already overcrowded; it introduces highly specialized courses into curricula allegedly already overspecialized. Further, as may be argued with considerable weight at the University, a course in state history would merely duplicate materials already adequately offered.

Again, if Illinois history is taught in the public school system, it is of prime importance that it be taught by well-trained, competent instructors whose historical knowledge is broad enough to avoid the pitfalls into which local historians so frequently tumble. Properly taught, the history of Illinois affords a splendid springboard from which to plunge into the entire stream of human history. The history of our state is exceedingly rich. During the seventeenth and eighteenth centuries the Illinois Country was a major point of conflict in the European struggle for control of North America; in the nineteenth and twentieth centuries the state was organized, populated, and developed as a result of nation-wide and world-wide forces, economic, political, religious, and psychological. State history taught against such a background with an intelligent and constant attention to the state in relation to the nation and to the world at large can become the most valuable, meaningful, and illuminating kind of history. If I misunderstood him not, it was this type of local history to which President Fox referred so eloquently last night. It is a history which can enrich and ennoble the life of every man. But state history taught without this broad vision is in serious danger of becoming a meaningless procedure of piling fact upon fact for the sake of facts. Of course, the antiquarian and the genealogist would gain satisfaction from such a course, and through their activities the historian often is supplied with important data in local history; but for the average student, state history taught in a vacuum is meaningless and uninteresting, and the effect of its teaching may be even dangerous to the spirit and the welfare of the nation.

An important factor in the development of the United States as a united nation has been the absence of narrow local pride and overpowering provincialism in those states which were formed and admitted to the Union after 1800. For whereas a citizen of one of the original thirteen states tended to be a Virginia, a Pennsylvanian, a Carolinian, or a New Englander before he was an American, a citizen of the newer states in the West tended to be an American first, and state loyalties were relegated to a secondary position of proper and necessary local self-respect. State history taught over a period of years without intelligent safeguards and constant attention to its broader aspects is likely to become an inbred flatterer of stiffnecked local pride, of snobbish provincialism, and of a particularism dangerous to the welfare of the nation and of ourselves. During and since the World War we have become increasingly aware of the discords, divisions, and antipathies engendered by history taught in the provincial manner and so debased as to become a cheap form of propaganda or malignant chauvinism. In improper hands, state history, perhaps to an extent even greater than with more general history, becomes a powder-magazine filled with a self-pride, sectional self-interest, and provincial smugness. Properly taught—as President Fox has demonstrated far better than I—it can be interesting, vital, broadly cultural, and conducive to national and international understanding and good will. The University of Illinois is not opposed to the teaching of Illinois history. Through state history it believes the history of the nation and of the modern world can be illuminatingly revealed. Given necessary added resources, the Department of History is entirely willing to undertake this additional task in a specific form. But it is keenly conscious, and it urges all others to be conscious, of the responsibilities involved.

AN ILLINOIS MARTYRDOM

By FRANK H. DUGAN*

FOREWORD

In Alton, Illinois, on the night of November 7, 1837, a mob of men attacked a small group defending a printing press, killed its leader, Elijah Parish Lovejoy, and threw the press into the Mississippi. The author felt challenged to discover just why they should kill the most brilliant scholar, editor and churchman in their community.

On first investigations the deed would seem to be merely the result of hatreds engendered by abolitionism to which most men were opposed at that time. However, the Alton Riots had deeper springs than mere antagonism to abolitionism. Editor Lovejoy was a Puritan, the descendant of men who had suffered death rather than admit to the slightest change of a single sentence of the Bible. To him, the words, "Liberty and equality" in the Constitution meant exactly that for all men, and he would print it with that meaning even if all men disagreed. Neither would he surrender his principles, he said, though the whole world should vote them down. To the easygoing frontiersmen, to the Kentuckians and Virginians of Alton such beliefs were rank heresy. That such a man should try to place the stamp of temperance or abolitionism on Alton through the medium of his paper, *The Alton Observer*, was more than they would endure.

The plan of this study is to follow the Puritan minority, led

* Mr. Dugan teaches History and Social Studies at Roosevelt Junior High School in Alton, Ill. The following paper is based on the thesis which he submitted in partial fulfillment of the requirements for the master's degree at Northwestern University in 1938.

by Lovejoy, through all of its trials as it came into an inevitable conflict with the majority, and further, to reveal some of the other underlying conditions in the nation, and especially in Alton, which gave rise to the Riots of 1837. The part which Puritanism played is herein more or less fully delineated. Moreover, it is established that without Puritanism the Riots could not have occurred, or have had such far-reaching consequences.

The writer feels deeply indebted to Professor I. J. Cox, of Northwestern University, for the valuable guidance which he has given in the pursuance of this study; to Mr. Paul M. Angle, of the Illinois State Historical Library, for his aid in exposing the spurious Lincoln-Lemen letters; and to Professor Theodore C. Pease, of the University of Illinois, for his criticism of the bibliography. Mr. Paul B. Cousley, editor of the *Alton Telegraph*, and Mr. Gilson Brown, attorney, made many valuable suggestions.

Mr. Cousley was most generous in presenting me with the key to the old files of the *Alton Telegraph* for 1836-1837. Due to the partisan nature of most later accounts of the Alton Riots, the author has relied mainly on contemporary letters and newspapers for his account, and so feels most grateful to the staff of the Chicago Historical Society Library, which provided him with an abundance of these materials, particularly the complete, original file of *The Alton Observer*, the Lovejoy anti-slavery organ, and with files of the *Alton Spectator*, *Western Pioneer*, *Genius of Universal Emancipation*, and *Genius of Liberty*. Acknowledgment would not be complete without reference to the efficient services rendered the writer by the staff of the Illinois State Historical Library, the Newberry Library, and the Hayner Library of Alton.

I. PRELUDE TO THE ALTON RIOT

All day Sunday, July 24, 1836, and far into the night a printing press lay on the Mississippi landing of Alton, Illinois. The captain of the steamboat *Palmyra* had unloaded it on Sunday, after its

Puritan owner, Elijah Parish Lovejoy, had declined to receive
it on that day.   The unguarded press lay on the landing till late
that night when suddenly the rugged bluffs, the silent river and
the lowland echoed to the sound of hammers on metal.   The river
then received the broken remains of the press.   Such was the
reception of Lovejoy's first press in Alton.[1]

The former editor of the *St. Louis Observer*, graduate of the
rock-bound college at Waterville, Maine, and of Princeton Theo-
logical Seminary, had been the object of tremendous hostility from
St. Louisans aroused to anger by editorial crusades opposing in

---

[1] *Alton Observer*, Sept. 8, 1836; Henry Tanner, *The Martyrdom of Lovejoy*
(Chicago, 1881), 87.

hard and biting terms their traffic in slaves, their grogshops, mobs, and easy-going churches. On the evening of July 21, 1836, a mob destroyed the *Observer* office, and drove Lovejoy from the city.

Such persecution steeled him in his determination to carry on his reforms. His life was one unbroken record of stubborn persistence in his principles. His was a profound conversion. He wrote in 1832: "The cry of the oppressed has entered not only into my ears, but into my soul, so that while I live, I cannot hold my peace." When his first press was destroyed because he would not allow it to be moved from the Alton landing on Sunday, he almost immediately set off by boat to Cincinnati to procure another, writing: "I have got the harness on, and I do not intend to lay it off except at His command." When a committee of St. Louisans warned him of the consequences of his anti-slavery editorials, he published his reply addressed to the people of St. Louis and told them that he could not surrender his principles, "though the whole world should vote them down." After being mobbed the first time, he wrote, "I have had the honor of being *mobbed* at last." He was then sure that he was on the right side.[2]

The reception of his press in Alton is not surprising. Alton was, in the summer of 1836, a boom town of loose and easy morals. It had its Tontine Row of coffeehouses and grogshops, a row of shanty-like structures sprawling back from the river landing about one-quarter of a mile below the painted Piasa Bird. It had its Sunflower Island just across the river which was a convenient spot to settle any quarrels that could not be patched up. It had its share of the riffraff of a river town in those days, free-negro stealers, gamblers and outlaws. Such people played cards, drank, fought, danced, and in groups openly paraded the streets on Sunday.

Of the Altonians, a part came from New England and New York, while the oldest settlers were from the South, particularly from Kentucky and Virginia. The New England people, the

---

[2] Joseph C. and Owen Lovejoy, *Memoir of the Rev. Elijah P. Lovejoy* (New York, 1838), 180-82.

newcomers, were regarded with distrust by the southerners. Their prejudice against "Yankees" was "unconquerable." They looked askance at people who refused a drink of whisky. They held in disfavor those who would not sit in on the local pastimes of seven-up or poker. They sneered at young eastern lawyers who brought law books into the courtroom. They were not tolerant of new ideas; they preferred the free and easy life of the frontier to the strait-laced morals of the Yankee reformer. In city politics they supported the party known as the "Mint Juleps," while the Puritan minority composed a group known as the "Teetotalers," sneered at by the *Alton Spectator* as the "Cold Water Society" and the "Sunday School Scholars." In 1836, the "Mint Juleps" elected John M. Krum mayor, and he gave voice to the prevailing attitude when he said in his inaugural address that he was all for the policy that "honey will catch more flies than vinegar."[3]

Alton was a town of bold, enterprising men, who sought to carve out their fortunes in town-lot speculations and river trade. In 1836, its people boasted loudly of its one hundred new buildings, of river front wholesale houses doing a business of from one-quarter to one-half million dollars that year, of business lots which sold for three hundred to four hundred dollars a front foot. With Alton located on the Mississippi near the mouths of the Missouri and Illinois rivers, some Altonians began to dream of a future city which would surpass St. Louis in the river trade and grow to be the great city of the valley. Many men flocked in from the East, forced to leave their families behind them because of the lack of houses. Steamboat captains took strangers on board for the night; otherwise it was said that they would "have been forced to take shelter among the bluffs and hills, or to take up with the soft side of a plank on which to rest their weary limbs."[4]

---

[3] *Autobiography of the Late Col. Geo. T. M. Davis*, published by his legal representatives (New York, 1891), 50; Kizzie H. Shifflett, *The Fifth Seal* [Springfield, Ill., 1922], 159; *Chicago Democrat*, Sept. 26, 1838; *Alton Spectator*, July 6, 1837.
[4] John Mason Peck, *A Gazetteer of Illinois* (2nd ed.; Philadelphia, 1837), 146-50; *Alton Telegraph*, Jan. 15, March 30, 1836.

The new England group proposed to make changes in the moral pattern of the town. Lawson A. Parks, friend of Lovejoy, who edited the *Telegraph* in 1836, advised licentious and intemperate immigrants to go elsewhere. "They may mingle with the herd that now infests the town and which must soon pass away . . . but will gain no foothold here." Colonel Godfrey and Winthrop S. Gilman, who owned the largest warehouse on the river front, had a fine church structure of native stone, with tall Gothic windows, erected on Market Street hill. From its pulpit a stern New England morality opposed all that the Tontine Row represented, and its rafters echoed to the voices of Elijah Parish and Owen Lovejoy, Edward Beecher, Peter Cartwright, Frank Graves, and John Mason Peck.[5] The New England Puritans also organized Sunday Schools and Sunday School conferences, set up temperance societies, and planned a merchants' organization which would refuse to ship or receive goods on Sunday. A. W. Corey, in 1837, came to Alton to establish headquarters for the *Illinois Temperance Herald*. Finally, Presbyterian clergymen of Illinois invited Lovejoy to come to Alton to set up a religious paper and pledged to pay all deficits incurred by it for a period of two years.[6]

In a bold and caustic manner the Puritan wrote of "divine truth, in all of its severity." He pointed his pen at the Eagle Tavern in connection with the death of a young man, citing the episode as an instance of the "long and dark catalogue" of victims of intemperance. He supported A. W. Corey when the latter published the names of St. Louis wholesale dealers in liquor, charging all these with being common criminals. Considerable apprehension was then felt by the temperance group for the safety of both the *Observer* and *Herald* as threats were made. In the case of a drunken murderer, he suggested that the man who sold the murderer the liquor should be brought to court. When the Panic of 1837 began to make its effects felt in Alton in the lessening of the number of steamboat arrivals, the scarcity of money,

---

[5] *Alton Telegraph*, May 11, 1836. This fine old church is now an Episcopal Church.

[6] *Alton Observer*, Nov. 24, 1836.

and the disappearance of town-lot buyers, Lovejoy laid it all at the door of greed, "that earthborn groveling propensity," as he called it. Bluntly he told the people, "Our nation cannot be trusted with riches," which lead them into the paths of sin, to Sabbath breaking, to slavery, and to intemperance. He, for one, was glad that their "town-lot bubble" had burst, he said.[7]

When the story was circulated that Lovejoy was pledged not to publish abolition articles in his Alton paper, he wrote an open letter in the *Telegraph*, stating that he would, from a sense of religious duty, oppose slavery on every "suitable occasion."[8] In 1835, he was a colonizationist; in 1836, he came to believe in gradual emancipation; in 1837, he advocated the immediate emancipation of the slaves. He regarded the question of the safety of emancipation as "conclusively settled" by the results of the West India emancipation. He knew slave conditions from having lived amidst them eight years in Missouri. He wrote in scathing terms of slaves sitting outside the church on the carriage box on Sunday, while their owners went inside to worship, of slaves denied an education or legal marriage, of families broken up and sold down the river, of church members, elders and ministers, "who connive at, or approve, or worst of all, practice the abomination of slavery." He loudly applauded David A. Smith, a Presbyterian elder of Huntsville, Alabama, who freed twenty-one slaves and brought them to Alton, in April, 1837; he was described "as a man whose Christian principles are strong enough to enable him to do right at the expense of his purse." He shouted to the skies that these men "are no longer property, but men!"[9]

Slavery had no legal status, no constitutional status, or indeed, no common-law status, in his view. The negro was "God's, only," and he denied "that man can hold *property* in man." The negro had a natural right to freedom under the law of God; hence slavery was nothing less than a "robbery" of men, body and soul. It

---

[7] *Alton Observer*, May 11, May 25, July 13, 1837; *Alton Spectator*, Aug. 21, 1837; Tanner, *Martyrdom of Lovejoy*, 100n.
[8] *Alton Telegraph*, July 27, 1836.
[9] *Alton Observer*, Feb. 9, Feb. 16, April 20, 1837.

deserved no respect whatsoever. This was the stand of a small but determined Puritan minority which backed the only anti-slavery paper in the frontier West. As of old, they believed that the law of God remained binding on rulers and people and was opposed to slavery.

Lovejoy was growing more bold in his denunciation of slavery. On the Fourth of July, while orators in the Market House and in Upper Alton's Grove were declaiming the traditional themes of liberty, he sat in his office and wrote an editorial:

> Alas! what bitter mockery is this. We assemble to thank God for our own freedom, . . . while our feet are upon the necks of nearly THREE MILLIONS of our fellow men! Not all our shouts of self-congratulation can drown their groans—even that very flag of freedom that waves over our heads is formed from materials cultivated by slaves.

He resolved to act and sent out a call on July 6, 1837, for a state convention to form an Illinois Anti-Slavery Society. This call was backed by the anti-slavery societies in Putnam, Will, Adams, Bureau, Jersey, Macoupin, and Madison counties.[10]

Lovejoy felt that his duty as a Christian required fearless opposition to slavery. He had listened in St. Louis to a minister preaching on sins, hinting of slavery, then passing over it in silence, with the pro-slavery congregation on the edges of their seats, intent for the bombshell that never fell. Lovejoy wrote:

> Had he ventured to denounce slavery as he had denounced intemperance, he never would have gone into that pulpit again. His church would not have endured such doctrine. . . . I should have done it at whatever risk. As a minister of the Gospel, *I* should not have dared to do otherwise. . . . I would willingly have given one year of my life to have stood on the vantage ground the speaker then occupied . . . and then to have poured upon their startled consciences the denunciations of God upon those who "oppress the poor and the needy." . . . I would have done it, though in so doing I had expended my last breath.[11]

---

[10] *Alton Observer*, July 6, July 20, 1837.
[11] *Ibid.*, Feb. 9, 1837.

The *Observer* printed the articles of people who disagreed with abolitionists. It printed the articles of "An American," a series of long essays attacking abolition. Neither the *Spectator*, *Telegraph*, nor *Pioneer* would print abolitionist articles; they printed only colonization articles; the *Observer* printed both. Its editor continually urged that both sides be heard; when he heard that a new organ had been established in Washington to defend the slave system, he wrote: "We are glad of such a movement as this. . . . Rather than it should fail, we will ourself become a subscriber. . . . But let us have done with mobs and all attempts to shut the mouths of freemen on the subject."[12]

With a grumble and a rumble Lovejoy's press spread the new gospel of freedom for all men over the prairies of Illinois. The *Observer* subscription list grew from 483 in January, 1837, to 1,700 by March, and to 2,500 in August of that year. Letters came in from Missouri, Kentucky, and Illinois applauding Lovejoy's brave stand; anti-slavery societies encouraged him. "If they drive you from Alton, I will take two papers from you instead of one," wrote one who described himself as not being a "whole hog abolitionist."[13]

The community became excited over the Puritan and his editorials. Speculators were indignant over the article entitled, "The Bubble Burst." Others saw back of the lessening of the river trade the pen of Lovejoy. Some accused him of desiring amalgamation of races. John Mason Peck and his Baptists were converted to the frontier spirit of intolerance and frowned on his uncompromising spirit. Peck entered in the *Western Pioneer* his "solemn protest" when Lovejoy advocated hanging leaders of pro-slavery mobs. Judge Bailhache of the *Telegraph* maintained a cool aloofness from all the *Observer's* quarrels. A letter in the *Spectator* of July 20, 1837, signed "Many citizens" denied Lovejoy's accusation against the Eagle Tavern and, mocking his grammar, bitterly denounced him for his "long and dark catalogue

---

[12] *Alton Observer*, March 16, April 13, May 18, June 22, July 20, July 27, 1837.
[13] *Ibid.*, April 20, May 31, July 13, Aug. 17, 1837.

of lies." The editors of the paper denounced him for his "new-fangled doctrines creeping into our city under the guise of religion" and threatening its peace and prosperity. A meeting of protest against the *Observer* was held in the Market House on July 11, 1837. Lovejoy replied in a published letter that he could not recognize that their meeting or any public meeting could dictate to the press. Freedom of expression, he declared, comes to us "from our Maker . . . belonging to man as man."[14]

On August 17, the *Missouri Republican* of St. Louis asked that action be taken against the Puritan. It urged that he had forfeited all claim to the protection of Alton or any other city because of his rash course. If action were not taken, immigrants would avoid this section, and trade with the South would cease. The *Alton Spectator* on July 20 also urged that action be taken against the *Observer*. So, on the night of August 21, Lovejoy was surrounded by his enemies at a secluded spot on the Hunterstown road. The plan was to send him down the river in a canoe. His bold stand compelled admiration, and he was released. After filling up on whisky, the same mob threw his press into Second Street and demolished it. Whereupon Lovejoy sent out a call for money to procure a new press, writing, "We need your help, and must have it or sink." From Illinois, Missouri, Ohio, and Kentucky, the response of small anti-slavery groups was instant; the voice of lovers of a free press was indignant. The reply was that the *Observer* should go on; the money was pledged. Another press was brought in. Soon ten or twelve men came and took it from the store of Reuben Gerry and Royal Weller and threw it into Piasa Creek.[15] The opposition was just as determined that the *Observer* should not go on.

Lovejoy wrote home: "Four-fifths of the inhabitants of this city are glad my press has been destroyed." He added that the leaders of the city blamed him for the disturbances, that the ministers were all silent but one, the righteous indifferent, and the

[14] *Alton Observer*, July 20, 1837; *Alton Telegraph*, July 19, Aug. 16, Oct. 11, 1837; *Western Pioneer*, March 29, 1837.
[15] Joseph C. and Owen Lovejoy, *Memoir*, 232-51.

riffraff ready to follow the leaders.   But he swore that he would never abandon the enterprise.   He laid all credit for his firm stand to the guiding hand of God.   He concluded: "If I am to die, it cannot be in a better cause."[16]

Lovejoy was now shunned by the majority of people.   Former friends cut him dead as they passed in Second Street.   In the stores and on the streets people were heard to remark, "Good enough for him" or "Served him just right," in reference to the destruction of the presses.   Men such as Colonel Benjamin Godfrey told him to his face that they were withdrawing their support from the *Observer*.   People marveled at his "stubbornness," and the topic of incessant conversation was inquiry as to the next action of Mr. Lovejoy.

In the midst of this state of popular feeling, the first Illinois State Anti-Slavery Convention met in Upper Alton on October 26.   Over two hundred had signed the call; only eighty-five came to the meeting and of these only fifty-nine remained to sign the Constitution adopted by the convention.   Across the prairies had flown the warning of leading men of Alton that the city would not allow abolitionists to set up headquarters there.   The proposal to found a state Anti-Slavery Society met with the silence of the grave in southern Illinois; the delegates came especially from Quincy, Galesburg, Alton, and other central and northern parts of the state, where New England Puritanism was strong.   Over the whole state the majority sentiment was against the abolitionists.   In January, 1837, a committee of the Illinois legislature, in reply to the memorials of southern legislatures denouncing abolitionists, had found: "These societies have forged new irons for black men . . . have scattered fire brands of discord and dissension among the different states of the confederacy; they have threatened the violation of the sacred rights of private property." The little anti-slavery societies of Illinois protested bitterly against this report.   In Adams County in July, 1837, the Society in its second annual report wrote:

---

[16] Letter of Oct. 3, 1837, Joseph C. and Owen Lovejoy, *Memoir*, 258-60.

We wish it known to those who are pleading for inalien-
able rights, that there are some in Illinois who are co-workers
with them, there are some who will not sacrifice their liberties
and freedom on the altar of slavery, though they may have
been offered thirty pieces of silver.

With one accord Illinois anti-slavery societies denounced slavery as a "sin against God" and a thwarting of the Declaration
of Independence.[17]

The convention met in the Upper Alton Presbyterian Church.
Lovejoy's invitation had limited the call to those who believed
slavery a sin and looked to immediate emancipation. However,
Edward Beecher, the President of Illinois College at Jacksonville,
had placed another call in the *Alton Telegraph* of October 18, to all
"friends of free inquiry." Beecher hoped that there could be
found through discussion some "great principles on which all
good men can unite." So, when he arrived late in the afternoon
by stage from Carlinville, he found a hodgepodge of men of all
beliefs claiming seats under his call. Even some of the avowed
press destroyers were included.[18]

Elijah Parish Lovejoy called the meeting to order. He was a
sturdily-built young man of medium height, soberly dressed in
frock coat and stock, his hair combed straight back in severely
plain fashion. His bearing was dignified; his manner of speech
was grave. With his firmly set jaw and piercing black eyes, he
bespoke a spirit of cool determination.

Gideon Blackburn, of Carlinville, was called to the chair.
He was not in full sympathy with the doctrines of Lovejoy. On
the morrow he was to be elected president of the convention, but
he was not one of this group in spirit or purpose. He told J. M.
Buchanan, of Carlinville, that he "would rather give $50 (or some
considerable amount of money, . . .) to assist in prosecuting those
who destroyed the press last summer, than $5, (or some very small

---

[17] *Alton Observer*, May 31, July 13, Aug. 3, Aug. 17, 1837.
[18] Edward Beecher, *Narrative of Riots at Alton: in Connection with the Death
of Rev. Elijah P. Lovejoy* (Alton, 1838), 1-29.

sum, . . .) to continue the paper."[19]

The secretary of the convention was the Reverend Frank W. Graves of the Lower Alton Presbyterian Church. It was he alone among the ministers in the Lower Town who gave the *Observer* his unswerving support. He held his church open to leaders of both sides and was fearless in his denunciation of the press mobs.

A natural leader of the convention was Dr. David Nelson, of Quincy, who had been successively an army surgeon under Jackson in the Creek Wars, a slaveholder and atheist, a Presbyterian minister, and President of Marion College, at Marion, Missouri. He had read an emancipation paper from the pulpit at Marion, for which effort a Dr. Bosley, a slaveholder, attempted to shoot him. He hid in a thicket for several days, then escaped the popular fury by moving to Quincy, Illinois. Here, he continued his efforts at emancipation, founding a Mission Institute and encouraging his young disciples to go into Missouri and carry away slaves. In 1843, Missourians crossed the river and set fire to the Institute buildings. That, however, only increased his endeavors. It was Nelson who had played a prominent role in the conversion of Lovejoy to the faith in 1832.[20]

One of the youngest men in the assembly was Owen Lovejoy. As secretary of the Madison County Anti-Slavery Society, he wrote the call that seconded the call of the *Alton Observer* for a state convention. As a student of theology in Alton, he was becoming thoroughly indoctrinated with his brother's ideas on emancipation. When Elijah fell a martyr to the cause, Owen took up the pen and continued the fight in the *Genius of Universal Emancipation*, published at Hennepin by Benjamin Lundy, and in the *Genius of Liberty*, its successor, published at Lowell, Illinois. He became a leader in the work of helping slaves to escape, and was indicted twice in the Bureau County Court for these activities.

---

[19] Letter of J. M. Buchanan to the Rev. T. B. Hurlbut, Feb. 16, 1838, quoted in A. L. Bowen, "Anti-Slavery Convention held in Alton, Illinois, October 26-28, 1837," *Journal of the Illinois State Historical Society*, Vol. XX, no. 3 (Oct., 1927), 354.

[20] W. B. Sprague, *Annals of the American Pulpit* (Philadelphia, 1855), IV: 676-88.

He led in the organization of anti-slavery societies all over northern Illinois, announcing his appearances in advance, and fearlessly spoke and went his way. He was a pioneer in organizing the Liberty Party in the state and finally carried the cause of emancipation into the halls of Congress where he was denounced and slandered by southern congressmen.

Another man of note in the convention was Thaddeus Beman Hurlbut, circuit rider, associate editor of the *Observer* and comrade of Elijah Lovejoy in all his trials. He was a graduate of Andover, was licensed to preach by Lyman Beecher, and was well schooled in the Puritan tradition. It was he who stood guard over Lovejoy's body the whole night through as the fallen leader's corpse lay in the counting room of the Godfrey-Gilman warehouse.

Among the friends of the *Observer* in the convention were the Reverend Thomas Lippincott, former editor of the *Edwardsville Spectator*, who played a prominent role in defeating the pro-slavery convention proposal in 1823; the Reverend Aratus Kent, known widely as the moral rock of Galena; the Reverend Jeremiah Porter of Peoria, who was soon to make the beginnings of abolition organization in Chicago; Edward Beecher, President of Illinois College, who so thoroughly indoctrinated that institution with anti-slavery ideas that Governor Duncan threatened to resign from its Board of Trustees; the Reverend Asa Turner, another of the "Yale Band;" the Reverend Joseph T. Holmes of Quincy, whose leadership saved the "Lord's Barn" in that town from the attacks of the pro-slavery people; and the Reverend Lucian Farnum of the Hampshire Colony Congregational Church at Princeton, a church that was strong in its support of the *Observer*.[21]

Almost without exception the fifty-nine sober Puritans who remained in Upper Alton to sign the Constitution of the Illinois Anti-Slavery Society were Presbyterian or Congregational ministers and elders. They had voiced their anti-slavery sentiments in

---

[21] A. T. Norton, *History of the Presbyterian Church, in the State of Illinois* (St. Louis, 1879), I: *passim*; *Proceedings of the Ill. Anti-Slavery Convention held at Upper Alton . . . 1837* (Alton, 1838), 23; also *Jour. Ill. State Hist. Soc.*, Oct., 1927, pp. 329-56.

the pulpits of Illinois before hostile congregations, but still they felt that God required their opposition to slavery.

Of the opposition, who claimed a right to seats under the Beecher call, Usher F. Linder, the Attorney General of Illinois, was a natural leader. Born in Hardin County, Kentucky, within ten miles of Lincoln's birthplace, he became a favorite among the southerners of Alton. He was a popular man in court, where he used his good looks, his six feet of manhood, his mastery of showmanship and ridicule to good advantage. At scarcely twenty-eight years of age such popularity had made him the Attorney General of Illinois. He had no use for "Yankee" doctrines and was especially bitter toward abolitionists whose work he felt, if successful, would surely ruin the South. He lived in Alton during the years 1836-1838, although the law required the Attorney General to reside at the capital.[22]

Edward Beecher, coming in late, found to his chagrin and surprise that none of those citizens of Alton on whom he had relied were there. Instead, he saw the loafers, the drunkards, the known destroyers of the presses, all claiming seats under his call. Seeing the pitfall he had dug for the convention, he tried to correct it. He proposed that those of the Lovejoy call be seated, and then that these determine the seating of the alleged friends of "free inquiry."[23]

The proposal of Edward Beecher led to wild confusion in the assembly hall. Men shook their fists, shouted, and cursed. Lovejoy resolved to act, was recognized, took the floor and declared flatly that the intruders had no right to seats. Attorney General Linder replied for the opposition; he insisted that his men were friends of free discussion and wished to meet the abolitionists on fair grounds, meeting argument with argument. Holding his ground, Lovejoy coolly told the Attorney General that he well

---

[22] Usher F. Linder, *Reminiscences of the Early Bench and Bar of Illinois* (Chicago, 1879), 19; Mason H. Newell, "The Attorney-Generals of Illinois," *Transactions of the Illinois State Historical Society for the Year 1903* (Springfield, 1904), 217.

[23] Beecher, *Riots at Alton*, 28-30.

knew the single and definite purpose of the meeting. "Can you as gentlemen interrupt us," he asked, "when you know you have no right here?" The opponents glared at him; the noise broke loose again; the Attorney General shook his fist at Lovejoy, "insultingly, . . . within about two feet of him." Lovejoy did not flinch or get excited, but coolly stared back.[24] The argument continued until Gideon Blackburn declared the meeting adjourned.

The Lovejoy men went off quietly enough, but outside in the churchyard the friends of "free inquiry" gathered together. Linder mounted a woodpile and began a harangue against Yankee practices and doctrines. He spoke of the new things they were bringing into the West; he laughed at their Sunday Schools; he sneered at their home missionaries; he scoffed at their temperance societies. Linder denounced Yankee abolitionists, getting in much ridicule of all of them, but of Lovejoy especially. To put a stop to the convention he and his "boys," as he called his group, planned to gather enough adherents to outvote the Lovejoy men. As he later indicated, during the Alton Trials, he did not propose that the community should be made to "swallow . . . any doctrine which this set of people may tell us is good for instruction, or profitable for salvation."[25]

The opposition crowd spent the evening drumming up new recruits. On Friday morning, October 27, when the convention assembled, Blackburn, the chairman, declared the proceedings of the previous day out of order. Events moved rapidly to the aid of "the boys" of Linder. The Church Board sent down a note forbidding the use of the church for any meeting given to "one sided discussion" of slavery. The note, implying that all should be admitted, struck consternation into the anti-slavery men. The opposition loudly cheered the reading of this note. The hall was filled with their members; a drunk fellow, Arthur Jourdon by name, stood by the front entrance and loudly asked passersby to "join our band." The names of 107 men, including many avowed

---

[24] Statement of Dr. Samuel Willard in Tanner, *Martyrdom of Lovejoy*, Appendix C, p. 220; Joseph C. and Owen Lovejoy, *Memoir*, 265.
[25] William S. Lincoln, *Alton Trials* (New York, 1838), 71-73.

enemies of the *Observer*, were enrolled on the convention record. There were the press destroyers, William Carr, James Rock, Frederick Bruchy and Josiah Nutter. There were those who boasted in later years that they had fired the shots which killed Lovejoy—Dr. Thomas M. Hope, Dr. Horace Beall, Dr. James Jennings, and James Rock. There were men who had opposed Lovejoy in the councils of the people, Usher F. Linder, John Hogan, Alton's state representative, Cyrus Edwards, candidate for Governor of Illinois, and John A. Halderman, who later led "border ruffians" into Kansas. Colonel Alexander Botkin requested the adoption of the Church Board's recommendation and was successful.[26] The friends of emancipation were outnumbered and outvoted. Beecher gained the floor and spoke to the convention. His words inflamed the opposition and injured the cause. Slavery, he told them, was not only sinful, but no constitution could protect it. If the constitution sanctioned slavery, then it was wrong and not binding on them.[27] This was his reply to the constitutional argument, the chief argument of Linder and his "boys."

Linder and the Reverend John Hogan were constantly taking the floor, making motions, using dramatic touches, all calculated to disrupt the serious counsels of the pious friends. Hogan, possessor of a quick Irish tongue, hopped up and down, never remaining long in his seat, his huge florid face provoking attention, and brooding no good for the Lovejoy men. The sharp shafts of ridicule he hurled at them aroused wild bursts of cheering from the "boys."

While Dr. Gideon Blackburn was elected president with seventy-three votes, Dr. Thomas M. Hope, who later boasted that he killed Lovejoy, was a close second with fifty-two votes. A committee of three, consisting of Edward Beecher, Asa Turner, and Usher F. Linder, was appointed to make resolutions for the convention. Beecher had his resolutions ready; when the committee met, Linder refused to sign them. He objected to them as im-

---

[26] *Proc. Ill. Anti-Slavery Convention, 1837*, 7-8.
[27] Thomas Ford, *A History of Illinois* (Chicago, 1854), 237-38.

practical; their "Scriptural grounds" irritated him. He had some of his own based on "high legal and constitutional grounds." These resolutions said that Congress had no right, the states had no right, the abolitionists had no right, to free the negro or interfere with a domestic system sanctioned by the laws and by the constitution. Beecher and Linder wrangled, grew angry; the former saw his plans going up in smoke. The "boys" had decided to gag Beecher's report and put through Linder's. Beecher, knowing that his group would be outvoted, realized that all was lost.[28]

In the convention, Hogan jumped to his feet, protesting a motion to consider Beecher's report. It was read, but not considered. Lovejoy, who saw that resistance was useless, kept in the background. The Linder resolutions were brought in and voted on. Meanwhile the pathetic Beecher again and again asked the convention if it would adopt Linder's resolutions without discussion. The reply he received each time was, "Yes, without discussion."[29] In this way the "boys" blocked the effort toward free discussion, and gagged the anti-slavery convention. The Linder resolutions were adopted, although the Reverend Graves, secretary, refused to record them. Linder's "boys" then quickly adjourned the convention.

The anti-slavery men reacted quickly to the defeat. They went to various houses that evening for consultation and prayer, and resolved to hold another meeting on the morrow. The following afternoon they gathered in the house of Thaddeus Beman Hurlbut. Here, in the long, stone house with ample fireplaces, the Illinois Anti-Slavery Society was born, while the "boys" prowled outside and tried to prevent this gathering.[30]

Lovejoy's band was not overcome; indeed, they were far from it. In them dwelt the spirit of Cromwell's men, the stiff-necked sectaries, to whom persecution was a stimulus; in fact, opposition

---

[28] *Proc. Ill. Anti-Slavery Convention, 1837*, 7-9; Linder, *Reminiscences*, 104; Beecher, *Riots at Alton*, 32.
[29] Beecher, *Riots at Alton*, 33.
[30] *Missouri Republic*, Nov. 30, 1837.

only steeled them in their resolutions to put the anti-slavery work through for their faith and their Maker.

The question of the re-establishment of the *Observer* in Alton provoked heated discussion; Lovejoy felt that all depended on the convention for his future support. Some suggested moving the *Observer* to Quincy; others said that the failure to set up another press in Alton would embolden mobs elsewhere and weaken the cause. Miles and Brook, Cincinnatians, told the convention that Birney had won in their city, and urged that Alton should not be deserted. Lovejoy felt that no other place would be safer than Alton. Driven from St. Louis, he had found Alton, in the free state of Illinois, no refuge, so would Quincy be one? On August 11, a great anti-abolition meeting had been held there; its people were not friendly to the cause.[31] All this was known by the convention.

In the midst of these remarks, Edward Beecher arose and addressed the assembly. His plea was for more courage. He told the gentlemen of Illinois that if they shrank from the defense of their rights, because the cause they advocated was unpopular, then freedom of the press was abandoned. In that case, all was lost. So he moved to re-establish the *Observer* in Alton. The motion was carried; Lovejoy was sustained and his spirits revived. A resolution stated:

> To shrink from maintaining these rights, because the cause advocated is unpopular, or because any do not believe all the principles advocated, is virtually to abandon freedom of the press forever, for never will it be assaulted except when it attempts to maintain doctrines which some, and it may be a large portion of the community disapprove and oppose.[32]

Elihu Wolcott, of Jacksonville, became president of the new Illinois State Anti-Slavery Society and Hubbell Loomis, H. H. Snow, Thomas Powell, Thomas Galt, and Aaron Russell were made vice-presidents. These deeply religious men, strong Puritans

---

[31] Joseph C. and Owen Lovejoy, *Memoir*, 262; Beecher, *Riots at Alton*, 44-45; *Alton Spectator*, Sept. 7, 1837.

[32] *Proc. Ill. Anti-Slavery Convention, 1837*, 11.

all, prepared a constitution, mentioning the power and glory of God with each successive thought. This constitution quoted the Declaration of Independence, but fell back mainly on God for support; its second article dedicated members' efforts to the "immediate abandonment" of slavery.[33] Edward Beecher, assisted by Wolcott, drew up a "Declaration of Sentiments." A message addressed "To the Citizens of Illinois" was also prepared. This boldly told the people of Illinois that though the anti-slavery men were a small band, a mere minority, still, "for that very reason our rights ought to be held the more sacred." Protesting vainly, they tried to explain that they were not for turning the world upside down, or for ruining society. Pointing out that at "no distant day" God would free the slaves, in the meantime they would stand on their rights and never yield to force.[34] In this declaration there was the spirit of the Puritans, and the Friends, who two centuries before had stood in pillories, had had their ears cropped, had wasted away in jail, or had suffered death rather than put bread in the mouths of priests or surrender their opinion regarding some phrase in the Scriptures. With this declaration, the convention adjourned.

During the days following the convention, the opposition in Alton was whipped into a frenzy by Hogan, Linder, Hope, Beall, and others. While one meeting held in the store of A. Alexander declared for the re-establishment of the *Observer*, another held in the Riley building declared that Lovejoy must quit.[35] Beecher, now that he saw clearly, was bound to see the thing through. He preached in the Upper Town at the Presbyterian Church on the Sunday and Monday following the convention, and on Wednesday in the Lower Town. His plea was for freedom of expression, for support of Lovejoy. One listener bluntly asked what was meant by the direction given in St. Matthew, "When they persecute you in this city, flee ye into another." Beecher replied that he

---

[33] *Proc. Ill. Anti-Slavery Convention, 1837*, 12, 21-23.
[34] *Ibid.*, 23-36.
[35] Wilbur T. Norton, *Centennial History of Madison County, Illinois* (Chicago, 1912), 62.

hoped things had not "come to this pass."[36] Future events showed that they had. On Wednesday evening, as he spoke in that rugged citadel of Puritanism, the Presbyterian church in the Lower Town, a brick was hurled through one of its windows. Henry Tanner in the upper gallery shouted "To arms!" The "militant friends" seized their guns, always kept at hand, formed a double line at the church door and escorted Dr. Beecher and the congregation safely home.

The people were indeed beyond control. It was in vain that "one of you" pointed out in the *Alton Telegraph* that muzzling the expression of one citizen might lead to muzzling another, until "all shall be compelled to hold their peace;"[37] that if such occurred, it would mark the end of Alton's greatness; that property would depreciate, and immigrants would avoid coming to the city. The persecutions of Lovejoy continued. On one day two drunks gained the inside of the Lovejoy home, a little frame house on the Hunterstown road, but were forcibly ejected by the Lovejoy brothers. On another day, a brick was hurled through a window, narrowly missing their sister. On another occasion, Elijah Lovejoy came home to find his wife and child hiding in the garret, where they had been driven by the stones of some ruffians. On still another day, he had to appear, rifle in hand, on his doorstep, in order to frighten mobsters away.

Under such circumstances, Lovejoy appeared at the *Telegraph* office one morning and presented a card to Judge Bailhache, editor, telling him that it was his resignation as editor of the *Observer*. He was "weary of contention," he told the Judge, and wished to do all in his power to restore peace in the community. He feared for the safety of his wife and child, he said. The judge jumped at this opportunity to allay excitement. Lovejoy left; Bailhache gave the card to William A. Beatty, his foreman. In a moment Frank Graves stepped in, asked to see the card and to show it to his friends, promising to return. The paper was delayed

---

[36] Beecher, *Riots at Alton*, 48-49.
[37] *Alton Telegraph*, Oct. 4, 1837.

for the resignation notice, but Graves did not return. He, together with Beecher and others, persuaded Lovejoy to stick. Now the drama began to unfold in earnest.[38]

Beecher, hoping to bring support to the oncoming press, and knowing that the influential businessmen of the city held the key to the situation, persuaded John Hogan and Winthrop S. Gilman to call a meeting of such men for the purpose of bolstering order in the city, and considering some grounds of compromise. The meeting assembled in the countinghouse of John Hogan and Company on Thursday afternoon, November 2, 1837. Cyrus Edwards, brother of Ninian Edwards, Illinois' third governor, was there, hoping to reap some added popularity, to ride with the majority, not to try to stay its course. Here also was John Hogan, short, stout, florid of face, and impetuous. He was a bitter enemy of the press defenders. Here came Usher F. Linder to oppose the Lovejoy group. These were the leaders of the majority. A queer assembly this; from the floor were seen the sober faces of Graves, Beecher, and Gilman, anxious, pleading now as they stood out against the majority. In desperation they submitted a series of resolutions that looked to the support of the editor of the *Observer*, not in approbation of his character or "course as editor," but in support of the principles of his right to "print and publish whatever he pleases."[39]

Linder and Hogan poured out barbs of sarcasm on the Gilman resolutions. Beecher, feeling a chill on his heart, argued for minority rights. He said he was "pleading not for men, but for principles."[40] His eyes met a wall of cold faces; not a voice was raised in support of the press. As he sat down, men were hinting that some things were worse than mob action. Stolid businessmen of old, but now with anger and fear in their eyes, were whispering about the dangerous fanatic abolitionist, Lovejoy, who

[38] *Alton Telegraph*, June 28, 1845; Shifflett, *Fifth Seal*, 188-89; Thomas Dimmock, *Lovejoy. An Address Delivered . . . at the Church of the Unity, St. Louis, March 14, 1888* [St. Louis, 1888], 16.

[39] *Alton Telegraph*, Nov. 8, 1837; Ford, *History of Illinois*, 240; Beecher, *Riots at Alton*, 52-54.

[40] Beecher, *Riots at Alton*, 59-60.

would pull down the structure of society around their ears, who sought, they said, to ruin their trade outlets in Missouri and down the river. This must never come to pass, they said. So they appointed a committee of Cyrus Edwards, chairman, John Hogan, Stephen Griggs, Usher F. Linder, H. G. Van Wagenen, Thomas G. Hawley and Winthrop S. Gilman to consider the resolutions and report to them on the following day.[41]

On Friday afternoon, the meeting convened in the Municipal courtroom, on Second Street, looking out to the mighty Mississippi. The object of all their deliberations was there; Lovejoy had come to make his last effort for freedom of speech and of press. The meeting got down to business first by voting Edward Beecher out of its active assemblage by a resolution admitting only citizens of Madison County. Rid of one thorn in its side, the majority looked askance at certain of the "militant friends" who had come in.

The committee had met and voted not to support the *Observer*. So now in the courtroom Cyrus Edwards, tall, commanding, elegant in dress, arose for the committee, called attention to the distracted state of the people, to the arming of parties, accused the Gilman resolutions of demanding too much concession from the majority, and said that there must be a "mutual sacrifice" by both parties. Therefore, he submitted that though Lovejoy had the right to publish a paper, it was not expedient that he do so at present. He presented the committee's resolutions, the fourth of which said that the editor of the *Observer* must "be no longer identified with any newspaper establishment in this city," as a necessity of "peace and harmony" in Alton.[42]

Lovejoy's friends protested this resolution. Winthrop S. Gilman arose and voiced his dissent to the resolutions, as he had done in the committee. John Hogan replied, spoke of Paul at Damascus, how as a matter of expediency, he had been removed from that city, let down its walls in a basket. The peace of the

---

[41] *Alton Telegraph*, Nov. 8, 1837. The proceedings of the meetings of Nov. 2 and 3 were printed in the *Telegraph*.
[42] *Alton Telegraph*, Nov. 8, 1837; Beecher, *Riots at Alton*, 73.

city required the removal of Lovejoy. Other men cried out that preachers should stick to preaching. Linder called for a vote on the resolutions. At this tense moment, Lovejoy, who had sat quietly, hearing it all, arose, came forward, asked to speak in his own defense.[43] By the bar within which the chairman sat he stood, and in a tone of deep feeling, addressed the people. He would not argue the question as presented in the report of the committee, he said. Looking at Cyrus Edwards, the chairman, with steady eye, he wondered that so great a man, candidate of the people for Governor of Illinois, could have brought himself to submit such a report, and, continuing, he told them:

> I do not admit that it is the business of this assembly to decide whether I shall or shall not publish a newspaper in this city. . . . I have the *right* to do it . . . subject only to the laws of the land for abuse of that right. This right was given me by my Maker; and is solemnly guaranteed to me by the constitution of these United States and of this State.

He pointed out to the tense audience:

> It is simply a question whether the law shall be enforced, or whether the mob shall be allowed, as they now do, to continue to trample it under their feet.

His duty, he told them, required him to stand by his principles. He was impelled to this course because he feared God more than he feared man. Furthermore, he had of late received a flood of letters urging him to remain as editor of the *Observer*.

> A voice comes to me from Maine, from Massachusetts, from Connecticut, from New York, from Pennsylvania; yea, from Kentucky, from Mississippi, from Missouri; calling upon me in the name of all that is dear in heaven or earth, to stand fast; and by the help of God, I WILL STAND.

In a softer voice of solemn accents, as a tense silence fell on the hearers, he said:

---

[43] Shifflett, *Fifth Seal*, 177. See Beecher, *Riots at Alton*, 85-91 for Linder's address. Lovejoy wrote what he could remember of this speech after the meeting and Beecher, who heard it, added the rest.

Why should I flee from Alton? . . . Where can I be safe, if not here? . . . Sir, the very act of retreating will embolden the mob to follow me, wherever I go. . . . It has been said here, that my hand is against every man, and every man's hand against me. . . . Against whom in this place has my hand been raised? . . . Whom of you have I injured? . . . Whose character have I traduced? . . . Whose business have I meddled with?

He paused; no answer came from the room. In a manner grave, his voice tingled with pathos, in the quaint language of a down-east Yankee of Maine, he told them of his persecutions. He told how on one day his wife had been driven to the garret through fear of the prowling mob; how the windows of his home were broken in by brickbats; how he was "pursued as a felon" through the streets. His wife would never recover from these shocks. He declared: "I am hunted as a partridge upon the mountains."

Again speaking in a quiet tone, as a hush fell on the audience and hard-faced frontiersmen began to shed tears and give way to visible emotion, he told them that he slept well, that all was peace within his soul, that he would in the service of the Lord make the supreme sacrifice. The contest must go on. He concluded: "Before God and you all, I here pledge myself to continue it, if need be, till death. If I fall, my grave shall be made in Alton."

When Lovejoy had finished, he left the room. Men were visibly moved; it looked for a moment as if he had carried the day. Dr. Benjamin K. Hart began to fumble with his glasses, half rose to go forward in defense of Lovejoy, then suddenly sank back, his face showing indecision.[44] John Hogan gained the floor and contended that Mr. Lovejoy should as a Christian and patriot abstain from exercise of abstract rights. He then said that he understood that Lovejoy had publicly pledged silence on the subject of emancipation. Frederick Graves rose and explained that Lovejoy had last winter asked for advice as to his course in regard to discussing slavery and was advised by a meeting of the friends to go ahead, there being at that time no public excitement about

---

[44] Shifflett, *Fifth Seal*, 181; Dimmock, *Lovejoy*, 15.

emancipation.[45] He asked Hogan if he remembered that Lovejoy had said at the first meeting in Alton that he would yield no right to discuss any subject. Hogan replied in the affirmative.[46]

Usher F. Linder rose and poured out sarcasm on Lovejoy. He asked if Alton's people would be dictated to by "foreigners;" he called the editing of the *Observer* a "usurpation" on the town; he objected to Yankee principles, to any paper whatsoever being established in Alton which preached abolition. They that will not compromise deserve nothing, he said.

As Linder spoke, the "friends" got up from their seats and filed slowly out of the room. Linder paused, saying that he was glad that they were leaving. The opposition soon voted on the resolutions, quickly agreeing to the one recommending that Lovejoy be no longer identified with any newspaper in the city, and dissenting from another that upheld the character of Lovejoy. The meeting adjourned, having thus paved the way for the riot soon to follow.[47]

II. THE KILLING OF LOVEJOY

By August, 1837, the opponents of the anti-slavery editor, Elijah Parish Lovejoy, had grown stronger in their bitterness toward him and his editorials. When a Market House meeting of protest failed to quiet him, when his plans for a state anti-slavery convention to be held in their midst went quietly forward, when he with relentless pen continued to denounce the easygoing northerners for their apathetic attitude toward slavery, and when on the other hand opposition leaders called out incessantly that

---

[45] In the summer of 1837 a wave of anti-abolitionism swept Illinois, resulting in anti-abolition meetings in several cities, and in Alton, in colonization meetings.

[46] *Alton Telegraph,* Nov. 8, 1837. The report of the proceedings of these meetings, in the *Telegraph,* is that of a paper pledged to strict neutrality over discussions of slavery.

[47] To the honor of Judge Thomas Hawley it must be said that he told this meeting that he did not care if the Abolitionists "paved the streets of Alton with their papers." He would not read them, but they had that right. Beecher, *Riots at Alton,* 95.

he was injuring their trade with other sections, the enemies of the *Alton Observer* felt that action must be taken.

A small band of the relentless opponents of Lovejoy made plans in secret to tar and feather him and set him adrift down the river in a canoe. The leaders of this group deserve some notice. Dr. T. M. Hope was constantly in political battle; later, during the Lincoln-Douglas debate in Alton, he embarrassed Douglas with questions, and shook his fist in defiance at the crowd which booed him. Dr. Jennings, a Virginian, loud in denunciation of the *Observer*, was later cut to death in a barroom brawl in Vicksburg, Mississippi. Dr. Horace Beall, forward in the persecution of Lovejoy, also intense in southern sympathy, was, years after the Alton Riot, burned alive by the Indians on the plains of Texas. Such men swayed the counsels of the intemperate young men who composed a large number in the city.[1]

Tar and feathers were provided; a canoe was located at a secluded spot by the river. The evening of August 21, the designated time, was now at hand. A bright moon shone down on the wild bluffs by the river, on the river road winding at their base, on the tall oaks and misty bottom lands. Over this rough path strode Elijah Parish Lovejoy, hurrying to Alton from his home on the road to Upper Alton, to procure medicine for his wife who was ill. The mission accomplished, he turned homeward. At a secluded place the band met him, followed him, threw clods at him. He did not hurry, believing that it was not for such a man as he was to flee. The band surrounded him; a line of masked men blocked the road in front of him. Some pushed up close and one cursed him. This was a signal for shouts of "Tar and feather him!" "It's the d—— abolitionist!" Lovejoy maintained his composure. Dr. Hope then told him of their purpose, that he was to be sent in an open canoe down the river, that he was not to return. Still Lovejoy faced the mob boldly. Such unexpected coolness evoked wonder from the group. Hope then told him

---

[1] *The Lincoln-Douglas Debates of 1858*, edited by Edwin E. Sparks (*Illinois Historical Collections*, III, Springfield, 1908), 503; Dimmock, *Lovejoy*, 23.

that if he would leave town with his family and goods the next day, he would not be molested. Lovejoy would not agree. Speaking in distinct accents, he requested them to take the medicine to his wife, answering no question as to what had been his fate. He then told them he was now at their disposal. "I am in your hands, and you must do with me whatever God permits you to do." For a moment intense silence reigned. Then it was broken, Dr. Jennings exclaiming, "Boys, I can not lay a hand upon as brave and defenseless a man as this is!" The line of men melted into the shadows; the mob retreated, and Lovejoy walked on home.[2]

After going back into town, the mob filled up on whisky, went to the building housing the *Observer*, threw the press into Second Street and destroyed it. The next day the opposition exultingly said, "Abolitionism is now at an end in Alton."[3] They were mistaken; the stubborn Puritans who composed Lovejoy's group brought in another press and on September 21, a group of ten or twelve men took it from the store of Reuben Gerry and Royal Weller and threw it into Piasa Creek. On October 28, 1837, the first Illinois State Anti-Slavery Convention, meeting in Upper Alton, resolved to support Lovejoy and bring in still another press.

By this time Alton was in a state of great excitement. Usher F. Linder, Lovejoy's most bitter opponent, then the Attorney General of Illinois, openly supported his "boys" in the determination to prevent another press from being set up. The sober Puritan group known as the "militant friends" of Lovejoy were just as determined to protect the fourth press to be brought to Alton. By November both sides were armed; both sides patrolled the river bank, waiting for each boat. The "boys" searched the most likely of them, while captains stood by in silence.[4] It was their avowed purpose to destroy the press as soon as it was found. The "friends" hoped to land it in secret, at night, if possible. They had guns stored under the floor of a warehouse. Someone

---

[2] Letter of Lovejoy to his mother, Sept. 5, 1837, in Joseph C. and Owen Lovejoy, *Memoir*, 232-34.
[3] *Alton Spectator*, Aug. 31, 1837.
[4] Beecher, *Riots at Alton*, 63.

of the opposition found the place; a group came to seize the arms. Joseph T. Holmes, a friend, hearing of this, arrived first, stood on the movable plank over the floor, folded his arms and gave the "boys" a very stern look as they appeared. They departed, one saying, "Holmes . . . looked as though he would as soon shoot a fellow as not."[5] The "friends" also had guns stored in Royal Weller's store and were fairly busy at the business of molding bullets. Many caught the militant spirit. The young son of Reuben Farley was amazed when he arrived home to find his father busy with the molds.[6] Edward Keating, lawyer, strolling along the river bank one night, met a patrol of the "boys." He remarked that a club which one carried was not much of a weapon, whereupon the man, dropping his club, whipped out a brace of pistols from under his coat. To this state of affairs the little community had come; business was suspended, as almost everyone talked about the stubbornness of the abolitionists, about their arming, and their intentions of defending the new press.[7]

While waiting for the press to arrive, Lovejoy met daily with Edward Beecher, Albert Hale, Thaddeus B. Hurlbut, Owen and John Ellingwood Lovejoy, at his home for prayer and consultation. He decided that the press could be defended by a small number of resolute men, especially if stored in the sturdy stone warehouse of Godfrey and Gilman. Gilman and Lovejoy met with Mayor John M. Krum at the Mansion House on the evening of November 6, to secure his sanction of the defense of the press. Genial William Harned, friend of Lovejoy and proprietor of the hotel, invited them there. Here also came A. B. Roff, Owen Lovejoy, Royal Weller and Edward Beecher. Alton's finest tavern was the scene of fervid argument.[8] Lovejoy insisted again and again that Krum should take command of the "friends" in defense of the press. Krum refused. He left the whole matter

---

[5] Tanner, *Martyrdom of Lovejoy*, 218.

[6] Stories told the author by the grandson of Reuben Farley, Rogers N. Farley of Alton.

[7] Ford, *History of Illinois*, 242.

[8] This fine old red brick structure with the dormer windows still stands on State Street Hill.

to the action of the city council. He told the Mansion House meeting that it had the right to organize a force in defense of the press, an "undoubted right." This, he was careful to explain, was not his advice as mayor; he was not advising as mayor![9]

At the insistence of Gilman, Krum requested the council to appoint special constables to maintain order. When the council met, it refused to act on the request. Instead, a Mr. King, a member of the body, moved that the mayor and council address a note to Lovejoy and his friends requesting that they give up the idea of establishing an abolition press for the present.[10] This motion was not acted on.

Now we come to the night of November 6. Gilman arranged that the press, coming from Cincinnati on the boat *Missouri Fulton*, should be landed at three o'clock in the morning, under cover of the guns of thirty of the "friends." The boat anchored at the mouth of the Missouri until midnight, then came on to Alton. Here boat hands brought the press ashore. It was placed in the third story of the warehouse. Lovejoy and Beecher took the first post over the press in the small hours of the morning. At dawn they were relieved and returned to the Lovejoy home. After breakfast they united in prayer, after which Beecher said his farewells and set off for Jacksonville.

The warehouse of Godfrey and Gilman in which the press was placed was a strong double building, built of native stone. It fronted on the river landing, running back one hundred feet, having no windows on the sides, the only entrances being the windows and doors on the south or river end, and the door on the north or Front Street end. In it at the time were hogsheads of sugar, salt, and tobacco on the first floor, and a large quantity of stone jugs on the third floor. The second story included a counting room. Opposite the southeast corner, distant about thirty paces, was a pile of boards and salt barrels; opposite the west side, a clay bank.

---

[9] Krum's testimony, Lincoln, *Alton Trials*, 36-41.
[10] *Ibid.*, 32.

The "friends" met at the warehouse in the afternoon. Lovejoy on "old John" rode over the hills to Upper Alton to rally them, especially his close companion, Thaddeus Beman Hurlbut. They drilled that afternoon at the warehouse, being commanded by Captain Enoch Long, a veteran of 1812. The town was quiet all day; they had no fear of being attacked that night, and all but some twenty odd went home. The rest sat around till nine o'clock telling stories.

With the evening, things began to wake up. Small squads of men began gathering in, and in front of, the coffeehouses and taverns of Tontine Row. In the Tontine Tavern a group of the "boys" ranged around the walls. William Carr passed around liquor to them. The jug circulated swiftly. A line was then formed out in front and took up the march on the warehouse. As they came near it, carrying flares, they stopped to pick up stones. Webb C. Quigley, a mere lad forced into the line, made a successful break for freedom, whereupon one cried: "There goes an abolitionist;" another cried, "Shoot him!" Now at the warehouse, they pelted its windows with stones, soon breaking out all of them on the Front Street side. James Rock came running down the hill, out of State Street with a keg in his arms. Guns were fired then from outside, as the hooting, howling mob of men, grown large now from the first mere thirty, began to gather courage.[11]

In the warehouse the little band of defenders, startled, sprang to arms, ranging themselves on all three stories. Ordered by Captain Long not to fire on the mob as long as it remained outside the warehouse, they watched the mob, peered out of windows, or threw its stones back. The mob charged the Front Street entrance with sledge hammers and rocks, breaking in the door, only to find it barricaded inside by hogsheads of sugar. As stones began to whistle through the third story, Reuben Gerry began to toss the stone jugs down at the attackers. The cry arose, "Shoot that fellow!" A mobster from the clay bank drew a bead on Gerry, but was in turn covered by Henry Tanner, from the second

---

[11] Lincoln, *Alton Trials*, 115-18.

story, after which both parties agreed to call it a draw.[12]

The "boys" went around to the river entrance, loudly calling on the defenders to surrender the press. Gilman opened the garret door of the second story and looked down upon the mob. They demanded the press again. By the light of the bright moon which hung low across the river, he told them that the Mayor had said for them to protect their property and they would risk their lives in doing so if necessary. On hearing this, William Carr raised his pistols to fire on Gilman. Some of the "friends" standing by pulled Gilman quickly away from the door.[13] Then the mob scattered to all sides. Firing commenced. A bullet plumped into the window sill close by William Harned. Outside, an answering shot dropped Lyman Bishop, one of the "boys," in his tracks. The "boys" retreated.

Henry West, a lawyer of Second Street, hearing the noise, hastened to the warehouse, intending to act as mediator. There he saw Dr. Horace Beall, Dr. James Jennings, James M. Rock, and others of the old crowd of relentless opponents of the *Observer*. Beall was shouting that he would like to kill every "damned" abolitionist in town.[14] Hastening into the warehouse, West sought out Gilman and urged him to give up the press, only to be met with Gilman's firm refusal, backed by that of Elijah Parish Lovejoy. Gilman asked West to go after Krum. The latter hastened on the mission.

The noise down by the river had meantime awakened the town. Little Mrs. Graves, invalid though she was, ran to the Presbyterian Church, of which her husband was minister, hastened to the bell tower, and rang the bell continuously for over an hour, hoping to rally people to the defense of the press. It was to no avail; none came to aid the defenders.

---

[12] Tanner, *Martyrdom of Lovejoy*, 226.
[13] Letter of W. S. Gilman to his brother, Dr. C. R. Gilman, Nov. 8, 1837, *Mississippi Valley Historical Review*, Vol. IV, no. 4 (March, 1918), 492; Harvey Reid, *Biographical Sketch of Enoch Long, an Illinois Pioneer* (*Chicago Historical Society Collections*, II, Chicago, 1884), 98.
[14] Lincoln, *Alton Trials*, 113; *American State Trials*, edited by John D. Lawson (St. Louis, 1916), V: 609.

Mayor Krum, with S. A. Robbins, justice of the peace, started toward the warehouse. On Second Street they met four men carrying the fatally wounded Bishop as "they might have carried a hog, one by each limb." Hastening, he met Solomon Morgan, running from home barefooted to be in time for the fun. Morgan stopped, recollecting that he had forgotten his gun, so sent a boy running for it. Krum asked him to go home. Morgan, by way of reply, asked Krum how he would like to have a "damned nigger" keeping company with his daughter. Krum, startled, replied that he would not like it. Together they hurried on. Arriving at the warehouse, they found a crowd of howling men in bell-crowned hats and long-tailed coats, firing into the building. Krum endeavored to get them to disperse. They, in turn, called out their determination to have the press, but suggested that they would retire while he went inside to tell the defenders of this determination. Krum then went inside. His efforts met with no more success than those of West. Going outside, he again admonished the "boys" that they were liable to penalties for their actions. His efforts met with the reply that he had better go home. At this instant a volley of buckshot whistled close by, some shot striking the mayor's hat. Whereupon he "decamped," accompanied by Justice Robbins, Judge Martin, Seth Sawyer and Edward Keating. Later, Keating approached the river door under cover of a white handkerchief. Admitted to the inside, he told the worried defenders that the warehouse would be blown up or burned in case the press were not given up. A third time the answer was that they would stick by their guns. A few would have surrendered, but Lovejoy only insisted the more strongly that they must protect the press.[15]

By now it was midnight and the moon was sinking in the west. A damp mist rose off the river. By the light of dim flares, the "boys" talked over their plans in hoarse whispers. Whisky had been brought into Front Street; their numbers had increased, and

---

[15] Tanner, *Martyrdom of Lovejoy*, 226; Lincoln, *Alton Trials*, 44-46, 115; *American State Trials*, 599-600; *Alton Spectator*, Nov. 9, 1837.

their courage had risen. Bishop was dead, and John Solomon "tolerably well peppered" with buckshot and this angered them.[16] They determined to burn the warehouse.

Several of the "boys" rushed toward the warehouse bearing a ladder. This they put against the east wall. Another followed with a flaming torch, climbed the ladder and set fire to the roof. Lovejoy and others rushed out the river door and fired on him, then returned inside. Soon the defenders heard the crackling sound of fire over their heads. Bert Loomis from inside the third floor punched out the flame and poured water on it, while the "boys" singled him out as fair game and fired heavily on him. A second time one of them mounted the ladder with a torch and balls of rags soaked in turpentine; again the defenders sent forth men to fire at the man on the ladder. Meanwhile Beall, Hope, Jennings, and Rock had hidden behind the pile of barrels to the southeast of the warehouse. As Lovejoy, Royal Weller and Amos Roff came out a third time to fire at the man on the ladder, they rose from behind their hiding place and fired a volley at these defenders. Weller received a shot in the leg, Elijah Lovejoy three buckshot in the breast.[17] Mortally wounded, Lovejoy ran back into the warehouse, climbed the stairs to the counting room, crying out, "I am shot! I am shot! I am dead!" When Hurlbut and Weller reached his side, he was breathing his last on the floor of the counting room.

Henry West came inside under cover of a white handkerchief, and pleaded with Gilman, Captain Long, and impetuous Henry Tanner that they give up the press with the understanding that the rest of the building would not be harmed. With the brave leader dead and the mob increasing in numbers, Gilman gave in, and allowed the press to be taken. The fire was put out, the press seized and broken up with sledge hammers, Josiah Nutter, one of the "boys," saying as he picked up a piece of it, "that it would do for painters to rub paint with."[18] Thus a fourth and last press

---

[16] Lincoln, *Alton Trials*, 118.
[17] *Miss. Valley Hist. Rev.*, March, 1918, p. 493.
[18] Lincoln, *Alton Trials*, 136.

The Attack on the Godfrey and Gilman Warehouse
From H. Tanner, *Martyrdom of Lovejoy*

was destroyed. Most of the defenders fled from the warehouse down the river bank as the "boys" fired shots over their heads.

Not all of them fled, however. While the "boys" were tossing pieces of the broken press into the Mississippi, Thaddeus Beman Hurlbut and Royal Weller placed themselves on guard over their lifeless leader. They reverently laid a napkin over his face and stood guard over his body the remainder of the night. Many mobsters came in to see the results of their work; young boys curious and frightened, and bitter enemies of Lovejoy. Dr. Hope gazed silently on the prostrate form, then offered to bandage the wounded leg of grim Royal Weller, which offer was instantly refused. One came to cry out at the dead Lovejoy: "Good enough for you. You should not have set yourself up against the people!"[19] Thus was revealed what the man of the majority thought was justice for the agitator and editor.

It was all over. Out on the Hunterstown road old Mrs. Delaplain, looking out, saw a riderless horse go by in the moonlight and exclaimed: "There goes old John! Something must have happened to Mr. Lovejoy!"[20] Thus young Owen Lovejoy and Elijah's widow had their first forebodings of catastrophe, when the horse came home alone. When daylight broke, the body was carried up Second Street to the accompaniment of the jeers and scoffings of the mob. There Dr. Beall, exulting over the night's work, shouted, "If I only had a fife, I would play the Dead March for him."[21] To the humble home of Lovejoy near Hunterstown the body was borne. There it lay all morning. There the young Owen, standing beside the remains of his brother lying in a plain pine box, vowed that he would carry on the cause that had been sprinkled with his brother's blood.[22]

---

[19] Letter of W. C. Quigley to the Rev. T. B. Hurlbut, Nov. 7, 1880, *Jour. Ill. State Hist. Soc.*, Oct., 1927, p. 356; *The United States Biographical Dictionary, Illinois Volume* (Chicago, 1876), 293; Norton, *Centennial History of Madison County*, 73.

[20] *Alton Telegraph*, Jan. 15, 1936.

[21] Tanner, *Martyrdom of Lovejoy*, 228.

[22] Norton, *History of the Presbyterian Church in Illinois*, I: 260; George W. Smith, *History of Illinois and her People* (Chicago, 1927), II: 184; Melvin Jameson, *Elijah Parish Lovejoy as a Christian* (Rochester, N. Y., [1907]), 95.

Even after Lovejoy's death the vengeance of the mob pursued him and his people. At the grave in City Cemetery, dug by a free negro, William Johnson, on that grey November day, only a few simple prayers were said, led by the Reverend Thomas Lippincott. The location of the grave was lost in after years, a road running over the spot. Rediscovered in 1864, the remains were removed to a place on the bluff overlooking the mighty Father of Waters. In that year Thomas Dimmock placed a scroll of New England marble over it. On it were inscribed the words, "Hic Jacet Lovejoy, Jam Parce Sepulto," which freely translated means, "Here lies Lovejoy, Spare him now in his grave," revealing the bitterness that persisted.

In January, 1838, various of the "friends" were indicted and tried for defending the fourth printing press. On November 7, 1848, Colonel G. T. M. Davis, then mayor of Alton, heard that plans were being made to attack the annual meeting held in the Lower Alton Presbyterian Church in commemoration of the death of Lovejoy. After ordering arms from the Alton arsenal and asking aides to be ready to protect the meeting, he then drove around the city in a sulky to see well-known leaders of the opposition. Stopping at their homes, he bluntly told them that he would not stand for a disruption of the meeting, that he would, in fact, fire on them with rifle and cannon, "if I had to apply the match to the latter with my own hand."[23] His excellent record during the Mexican War was well known. The meeting was not molested. Thus the old hatreds persisted over the memory of a man so disliked that no friendly judge could be found until 1847, before whom his estate could be taken for settlement.[24]

III. THE AFTERMATH OF THE ALTON RIOT

The Alton Riot was over and the little town returned to its regular way of life. A grave on the bluff, a silent stone building

---

[23] George T. M. Davis, *Autobiography*, 311-14.
[24] *Alton Telegraph*, Nov. 8, 1937.

with empty windows, and bits of type scattered in the streets were mute witnesses that the *Alton Observer* was silenced.

There were voices of both acquiescence and protest. At Springfield, the papers merely printed Mayor Krum's official statement of the Riot, reproduced from the *Alton Spectator* of November 8, 1837, but over at Jacksonville, Illinois College, that stronghold of abolitionists, seethed with anger at the killing of Lovejoy. Archer Herndon, of Springfield, father of young Billy Herndon, ordered his son home from Jacksonville, saying that he would not have him grow up "a damned abolitionist pup" at Illinois College. Governor Duncan, while condemning mob violence, thoroughly disapproved of Lovejoy and his radicalism.[1] The popular sentiment ran against the editor, the *Alton Telegraph* and *Western Pioneer* printed only a short notice of the Riot, and throughout the state the press seemed willing to give the event a quiet burial. On the other hand, the *Peoria Register* spoke out boldly against the action of the Alton mob, asking, "Was it for this our fathers periled their lives and fortunes?"[2]

The little anti-slavery groups of Illinois voiced their protests at indignation meetings. In Bureau County, at the little town of Princeton, such a group poured its contempt on Mayor Krum and the Alton Council for its conduct "in relation to the late Alton mobs," and for refusing freedom of the press to a minority, "however small." They invited the friends of the *Observer* to meet in Princeton for their conference concerning the establishment of an anti-slavery paper in Illinois.[3]

The news of the Alton Riot threw New England into a debate intense in its fierceness. In a Faneuil Hall meeting James T. Austin, Attorney General of Massachusetts, declared that Love-

---

[1] Albert J. Beveridge, *Abraham Lincoln, 1809-1858* (Boston, 1928), I: 226; Elizabeth Duncan Putnam, "The Life and Services of Joseph Duncan, Governor of Illinois, 1834-1838," *Transactions of the Illinois State Historical Society for the Year 1919* (Springfield, 1920), 159-60.

[2] *Chicago Democrat*, Nov. 18, 1837; *Alton Telegraph*, Nov. 8, 1837; *Western Pioneer*, Nov. 11, 1837; Beveridge, *Lincoln*, 226 ff.; Tanner, *Martyrdom of Lovejoy*, 167.

[3] *Alton Observer*, March 1, 1838 (printed in Cincinnati).

joy "died as the fool dieth," and that the Alton mob was an "orderly" group quite like the famous band that threw the British tea into Boston Harbor. In reply, Wendell Phillips invoked the spirits of the Revolutionary Fathers to rebuke the insult to free speech and press.[4] Phillips argued that Lovejoy stood well within his constitutional rights in defending his press.

The presses of New England poured forth contempt on the people of Alton. "Alton wished to please the slaveholders" so her people killed Lovejoy, said the *Boston Cabinet*. The *Massachusetts Lynn Record* asked: "Who but a savage, or cold-hearted murderer would go now to Alton?"[5] The *Cincinnati Journal* called out in feigned fear: "Alton! ! . . . Blood is on thy garments. Liberty has found a grave in thy bosom. But hush—speak not —a mob is on the throne."[6] Grave concern for the freedom of the press and for minority rights was also expressed.

Across the Ohio, in Kentucky, in Tennessee, in fact, throughout the South, the Riot was deplored. Most southern organs, however, said that Lovejoy had received what he deserved, because he had disregarded the excited state of public opinion, because he had plotted against the peace of society, thereby endangering the Union. The *Missouri Republican* said that he who excites a "tempest" should be the first to suffer.[7]

The question as to the rights of abolitionists had perplexed the country for several years. Some argued that they had no rights which the majority was bound to respect. Others said that they had all the rights of free speech and press, even though they were but a small minority. Many communities, however, denied them the exercise of free expression. The Alton Riot had

---

[4] Carlos Martyn, *Wendell Phillips: the Agitator* (New York, 1890), 92-102; *World's Famous Orations*, edited by William Jennings Bryan (New York, 1906), VIII: 222-30.

[5] Joseph C. and Owen Lovejoy, *Memoir*, 330, 331.

[6] Tanner, *Martyrdom of Lovejoy*, 163-64.

[7] N. Dwight Harris, *A History of Negro Servitude in Illinois* (Chicago, 1904), 96; M. K. Whittlesey, "Elijah P. Lovejoy," *Magazine of Western History*, Vol. VI, no. 3 (July, 1887), 231; John B. McMaster, *History of the People of the United States* (New York, 1906), VI: 477.

forced the question into the national forum; the trials which followed the Riot were watched by conscientious citizens with great concern. They saw that the court could by disapproval of the press destroyers strike a blow for freedom of the press and for minority rights.

In this expectation they were doomed to disappointment. The Alton Municipal Court convened on January 16, 1838, and first brought to trial, not the destroyers, but the defenders of the press. The indictment charged that Winthrop S. Gilman, owner of the warehouse from which the Lovejoy press was taken to be destroyed on the night of November 7, 1837, and others, had been guilty of an unlawful defense of property in "violently" resisting an attempt made to break up and destroy a printing press. The indictment cited them as violators of Section 114 of the Illinois Criminal Code, which stated: "If two or more persons actually do an unlawful act, with force or violence, against the person or property of another, with or without a common cause of quarrel, or even do a lawful act in a violent and tumultuous manner; the person so offending shall be deemed guilty of a riot."[8]

William Martin was presiding judge of the court. The trial was held in the municipal court building on Second Street. Francis B. Murdock was the prosecutor and was assisted by Usher F. Linder, Attorney General of Illinois. Linder was a bitter enemy of Lovejoy and his group. With the aid of his "boys" he had succeeded in disrupting the first Illinois Anti-Slavery Convention, held in Upper Alton, had backed the town meeting of November 3, 1837, in its resolutions that Lovejoy discontinue his paper, and had given his approval to the destruction of the press on November 7. Linder's request that he be allowed to aid the prosecution was backed by a petition of about sixty Altonians. They were determined to put the final stamp of disapproval on Puritanism and the friends of the *Observer*.

---

[8] *The Revised Code of Laws of Illinois* (Vandalia, 1827), 146-47; *American State Trials*, V: 535; Lincoln, *Alton Trials*, 6. Lincoln, son of Governor Levi Lincoln, of Massachusetts, was practicing law in Alton at this time.

For the defense were George Trumbull Moore Davis and Alfred Cowles. Davis later had a distinguished record in the Mexican War; was successively Secretary to General Quitman, Civil and Military Governor of Mexico, Mayor of Alton, Chief Clerk of the United States War Department, and Editor of the *Louisville Courier.* He was a personal friend of Daniel Webster, Henry Clay, John C. Calhoun, Stephen A. Douglas, and Abraham Lincoln.[9]

Alfred Cowles had an unquenchable love for the liberty that is American, the liberty to speak and write freely. He was not a politician,[10] but he was in sympathy with abolitionism. Neither Cowles nor Davis, however, had any connection with the Lovejoy group or with abolitionism.

The defense requested and secured a separate trial for Winthrop S. Gilman. Murdock and the Attorney General brought forth in the opening addresses to the court the remarkable argument that the statutes of Illinois had repealed the old common-law right of self defense of property, that a man's house was no longer his castle.[11]

The question arose as to the legal sanction the press defenders had secured. Witnesses testified that they did have legal sanction. Krum asked to be heard and testified that Lovejoy had "repeatedly" called on him to command a force of militia to defend the press, that he had declined to do so, but had told Gilman that he could defend his property with force, if necessary. He had also told the defenders that they had a legal right to armed defense of the press, the very night of the Riot. He also said that he had called on the city council to protect the press, but that they had failed to act.[12]

---

[9] *American State Trials*, V: 533n.

[10] J. F. Snyder, "Alfred Cowles," *Transactions of the Illinois State Historical Society for the Year 1909* (Springfield, 1910), 169.

[11] *American State Trials*, V: 536-37. The statement referred to was Section 114 of the Illinois Criminal Code. Also indicted were Enoch Long, Amos B. Roff, George H. Walworth, George H. Whitney, William Harned, John S. Noble, James Morse, Jr., Henry Tanner, Royal Weller, Reuben Gerry and Thaddeus B. Hurlbut.

[12] *American State Trials*, V: 552-53; Lincoln, *Alton Trials*, 38-41.

G. T. M. Davis, opening for the defense of Gilman, argued that the defenders of the press had a constitutional right to defend their property. Boldly he told the court: "I bid defiance to the statute the prosecutor has produced, and laugh to scorn the indictment he has read to you." Cowles, who appeared next, pointed out that Gilman was defending liberty of the press against the "unbridled lawless violence" of its enemies.[13]

Linder replied for the prosecution. In true frontier fashion this master of dramatics and showmanship paraded the character of the Puritan "militant friends" of Lovejoy before the jury. He laughed at rotund William Harned, their captain; he spoke in scorn of their marching and counter-marching "up in the garret of a warehouse, at dead of night." He called Lovejoy an "alien to our laws," the doctrines of his followers "fiendish." These men, he said, were defending "a press brought here to teach rebellion and insurrection to the slave; to excite servile war; to preach murder in the name of religion." In scorn he asked:

> Is this the age when virtue, religion and morals are to be forced upon us by the strong arm of power? . . . When by muskets and bayonets, we are to be compelled to swallow, whether we will or not, any doctrine which this set of people may tell us is good for instruction, or profitable for salvation?

He told how when the Yankees had appeared to be carrying all in their road to success the "boys" had wrecked the anti-slavery convention. "It happened that these Western boys knew a thing or two . . . and so they got together and outvoted them [the Yankees], and the convention blew up in smoke. It was a farce." This was the argument of the Attorney General of Illinois, prosecuting a man for defending a printing press.[14]

In the end, the defense having proved that Gilman stood well within the bounds of his constitutional rights, the foolish trial came to an end. Gilman was acquitted, and a *nolle prosequi* entered against the other press defenders.

---

[13] *American State Trials*, V: 568, 572.
[14] Lincoln, *Alton Trials*, 71-81; *American State Trials*, V: 579-87.

The attackers of the press were tried next.[15] They were arraigned on Friday, January 19, 1838, with Mr. Cowles and Mr. Murdock appearing for the state; Attorney General Linder, Seth T. Sawyer, and Junius Hall, for their defense. Brought to the bar were all the old enemies of the *Observer*, Dr. Horace Beall, William Carr, James Rock, Josiah Nutter, John Solomon, Frederick Bruchy, Solomon Morgan, Jacob Smith, David Butler, and Levi Palmer. Dr. James Jennings was indicted, but failed to appear; Henry West testified that Jennings had "taken French leave."

It was impossible to secure an unbiased jury to try the press attackers. The abolitionists in Alton, a small minority, were hated by the majority who were in full sympathy with the mob of November 7, 1837. Many citizens were challenged, but rejections could not go on forever, and in the end, a biased jury was sworn. Its foreman, Colonel Alexander Botkin, was an avowed enemy of Lovejoy, and had taken a leading part with the group opposing him.

Before such a jury the trial of the rioters was heard. Henry West, lawyer of Second Street, and Joseph Greeley told how the "boys" had planned for days to seize the press from the boat before it could be landed, and to destroy it. Enemies of the *Observer* were identified among those indicted as having been present at the time the press was destroyed, but no witnesses would say who fired the guns, nor would they say which men broke up the press. Some had seen a crowd gathering in a coffeehouse, or overheard hostile remarks against the abolitionists, but beyond this, they became vague in their utterances.

In his address to the jury Francis B. Murdock made for the state a strong appeal for the conviction of those who had smashed the press. Junius Hall and Seth T. Sawyer followed with pleas for the defense. Then before the crowd which packed the courtroom "General" Linder arose in defense of the rioters, and held both audience and jury spellbound. He defied the prosecution to prove

---

[15] Lincoln, *Alton Trials*, 83-158; *American State Trials*, V: 590-644.

that anyone did enter the warehouse, or destroy the press. While the partisan crowd nodded approval, he declared that an honest jury would not convict a man for the " 'cut of his coat,' or because he is seen in a coffeehouse, or because he happens to fall into what the gentleman may call bad company." Linder complimented the opponents of the Yankees as being real democrats; he posed as a hater of the well-born and well-bred, and wanted them all to know that he was a humble democrat.

Linder alluded to Cowles who was to make the closing speech for the prosecution: "You will be addressed in the cold and chilling expression of puritanical feeling, and the severe language of the law." He told the court that as he came down to the courtroom that day, he had gazed on the mighty Mississippi as it rolled by, had then hoped and felt that the address of Cowles "would meet with the same fate in the warm hearts of this honest jury" that the ice on the river finds when it is borne southward to a warmer atmosphere. In such a manner Linder defended the press destroyers.

Alfred Cowles next arose and stood before the same bar before which Lovejoy had made his last plea in the defense of his right to speak and print as an American citizen. Calmly and eloquently, he built up the several severe counts of the case against the "boys." He remarked that "the whole current of the mighty Mississippi" could not wash away the stain on the city of the bloody work of November 7. He told them that while Lovejoy was dead, and could not again speak, through his press, of "broken laws" and a "violated constitution," they could, by disapproving of the mob, cause that press from its watery grave to speak "trumpet-tongued" again. He pointed out that he was no abolitionist, but was an advocate of a free press for all. Boldly he stated that the fate of the city hinged on the decision of the jury. If they decided in favor of deeds of violence and murder, he asked, "Then, who will stay, or come among us?"

Cowles spoke for all real Americans, for all lovers of liberty, when he concluded that abolitionists had all the rights of citizens.

"Let abolitionists think, if they please; let them speak if they choose; let them print if they will. Freedom of thought is the birth right, and freedom of speech the charter of every American citizen."

The trial had taken up the entire day and then lasted until late at night. No one could be identified who had fired the fatal shots which killed Lovejoy and Bishop; the partisan jury regarded the casualties as a "stand off." Past midnight on January 20, 1838, Alexander Botkin, the foreman, returned for the jury a verdict of "not guilty." This ended one of the greatest mistrials in the history of Illinois.

As Cowles had prophesied, the press could not be silenced. The *Alton Observer* was re-established, this time in Cincinnati; its first number appeared December 28, 1837. In Illinois, Thaddeus B. Hurlbut and Owen Lovejoy planned to bring the paper back to Alton. Other abolitionists were not satisfied with the lack of a locally printed anti-slavery paper. Such a paper soon appeared. In July, 1838, Benjamin Lundy, grown old and gray in the cause of emancipation, and having been burned out in Philadelphia, started for Illinois. He was moved by the murder of Lovejoy to come out to the prairie state to "fill the gap" caused by the destruction of the *Observer*. On an old and battered hand press, in a little frame shack at Lowell, Lundy with the aid of John Ellingwood Lovejoy and Owen Lovejoy, brothers of Elijah, and assisted by Zebina Eastman, printed the last *Genius of Universal Emancipation.*[16] Grown cautious from experience, the editors addressed and circulated the paper from Hennepin, and hoped that the enemy would not find the press at Lowell. When Lundy died, Eastman and the Illinois Anti-Slavery Society took up the torch and with a new paper, the *Genius of Liberty*, intoned as "first principles" those principles of Elijah Parish Lovejoy, as stated in the *Alton Observer* on July 20, 1837.[17] The *Genius of Liberty* grew into the *Western Citizen*, and so the press of the anti-

---

[16] George A. Lawrence, "A Pioneer of Freedom, Benjamin Lundy," *Transactions of the Illinois State Historical Society for the Year 1913* (Springfield, 1914), 49.
[17] *Genius of Liberty*, Feb. 27, 1841.

slavery group of Illinois was never silenced.

Meanwhile from the abolitionist pulpits of New England came unceasing denunciation of the murderers of Lovejoy. The preachers began to build up in the minds of the congregations the idea that Lovejoy was a martyr. The Reverend Luther Lee called on ministers of the Gospel everywhere "to bring the dead body of the Alton martyr into their meeting houses, all gory in its blood, and lay it down before all the people that they may look upon it and be filled with indignation and horror."[18] Anti-slavery societies and abolition churches made the most of this opportunity, trumpeting a song whose chorus was the "Alton outrage," and its central theme the martyrdom of Lovejoy to the cause.

Preachers worked the martyr bellows; anti-slavery groups protested; in little schoolhouses indignation meetings proceeded; papers with black borders circulated, while new converts listened to a once shameful heresy now with quiescent minds. It was as Dr. Channing had written to abolitionists everywhere: "Mr. Lovejoy, had he succeeded in his defense, could not have accomplished his purpose. . . . Happy was it for our cause that under such circumstances he fell."[19] Thus the news of the Lovejoy murder roared through New England, leaving anti-slavery converts in its wake in every town.

John Mason Peck, editor of the *Western Pioneer*, in Upper Alton, could not agree that Lovejoy was a martyr. Lovejoy was to him only a dangerous agitator. Looking backward to the Riot, he boasted: "We took the calm course. . . now look at the results. Moral influence, religion, temperance, order, respect for law . . . have all been gainers. . . . A revival in most churches and a spirit of good feeling amongst all parties" were proofs to him that all was well in Alton, now that abolition agitation was silenced. He urged that mobs be treated with soft words, not denounced, for "a soft answer turneth away wrath." Many other leaders in Illinois, including Governor Joseph Duncan, felt the

---

[18] Luther Lee, *Address Delivered in the Methodist Church, Fulton, New York, December 3, 1837* (New York, 1838), 4.
[19] *Advocate of Peace*, no. 7, Aug., 1838, 66.

same way as Peck, and vehemently denied that Lovejoy was a martyr.[20]

In the following years, it seemed that the prophecy of Alfred Cowles had become true. Many of Alton's most distinguished men moved away. Immigration to the city practically ceased with the low reputation the city acquired in the East. Scarcely two or three of the older business houses of 1836 remained in Alton by 1848. It seemed to many as though a curse was on the town, not to be lifted for half a century. In time, Alton's editors and Alton's people were reduced to mere stammerings of bitter recriminations under the impact of scorn so deeply felt. On one hand, said Judge Bailhache, the slave states accuse us of being the "head of abolitionism" in this state; on the other, we are subject to "a systematized attack on the city by abolitionists" for being the place of an unfortunate riot.[21]

Slowly but surely as the years passed by, Altonians began to change their attitude of intolerance toward abolitionists. The year 1845 marked the turning of the tide. In that year, the Illinois Anti-Slavery Convention met again in Alton; this time it was not molested. In 1848, a premeditated attack on the abolitionists' meeting to observe the anniversary of Elijah Lovejoy's martydom was nipped in the bud by Colonel G. T. M. Davis, the mayor. And in 1860, during the Lincoln campaign, Congressman Owen Lovejoy came back to Alton to make a political speech. At the old city hall during the whole of a long evening, he held his audience with his compelling oratory. Coming to the end of his address, he told his hearers that this was not the time nor the place to speak of his brother or for the cause for which he died, but "as for his *cause*, time will vindicate that as surely as God lives and reigns."[22] He remarked on the sweet influence of his brother's life on those who followed him. He declared: "The blood of my brother, slain in these streets, ran down and mingled

---

[20] *Western Pioneer,* June 1, 1838; *Trans. Ill. State Hist. Soc., 1919,* 160.
[21] Norton, *Centennial History of Madison County,* 74; *Alton Telegraph,* June 28, 1845.
[22] Jameson, *Lovejoy,* 102.

with the waters of the mighty [Mississippi]."[23]   He quoted the
poet:

> The Avon to the Severn runs
> The Severn to the sea—
> And Wickliffe's dust shall spread abroad
> Wide as the waters be.

---

[23] John Moses, *Illinois, Historical and Statistical* (Chicago, 1889), I: 421; *Alton Telegraph*, Nov. 6, Nov. 8, 1938.

RICHARD J. OGLESBY: FORTY-NINER

HIS OWN NARRATIVE

Edited by MILDRED EVERSOLE*

INTRODUCTION

The cry of "GOLD" near Sutter's Fort in California on January 24, 1848, heralded the fact that James W. Marshall had found particles of the glistening metal in the tailrace of a sawmill. When the story of that momentous discovery was related in San Francisco shortly afterward, scenes of wild excitement occurred. And as the news spread across the country and across the water, a feverish desire to share in these new-found riches seized upon thousands of people. The tale of Marshall's discovery had hardly been told before the big parade of ships and wagons started from the four corners of the earth, all bound for the same objective. By the end of 1849, the movement had become one of the greatest migrations in history.

Among those of this country who made the long journey to California overland, Illinois was well represented. It became customary for prospective emigrants of a town or community to organize a company, draw up rules for the conduct of members, elect officers, and make plans for equipment and supplies for the journey. Some of these groups had fifty or a hundred or more members, but many smaller parties also took to the road. It is true that trails had been broken—the Mormon, Oregon, and Santa Fe were some of the better known ones—but the long trek across the plains, often among hostile Indians, was still a decidedly hazardous undertaking.

---

* Assistant Editor, Illinois State Historical Library.

Among the Forty-Niners who started out from Illinois was a young man who later became one of the state's most prominent citizens. Richard J. Oglesby had been admitted to the bar in 1845 and was just embarking on a legal career in Sullivan, Illinois, when the Mexican War began. He served as a first lieutenant of the 4th Illinois Volunteers in this conflict and at its conclusion again resumed the practice of law. But at the age of twenty-five his career as an attorney was interrupted again. This time he was a victim of "gold fever." In the spring of 1849, Oglesby was one of a group of nine men who left Decatur to seek their fortunes in Sacramento.

In the letter printed below—taken from the *Illinois Daily Journal* of October 23, 1849—he describes the experiences of this party in its two thousand mile journey westward. Young Oglesby and his companions arrived in California ahead of most of the emigrants from the Springfield region. During the course of their trip, he had discovered that many of the rumors circulated regarding the West were erroneous. His letter was written, therefore, to give the people back home a firsthand account, "in plain style," of the conditions he found on the long jaunt to the Golden State.

Oglesby was well repaid for making the trip. Within three days after his arrival at Sacramento, he returned the $250 which he had borrowed to pay his expenses on the journey and had almost double that amount left. Though during the course of the two and one-half years he remained in California, he lost a total of some five thousand dollars in a fire and in a bank failure, he still had almost that much in gold when he returned to Decatur in 1851 to resume the practice of law.

A political career was now opening up for the young miner-lawyer. He had previously demonstrated his ability as a stump speaker in Whig campaigns, and he became a member of the new Republican Party when it was organized. He was elected state senator in 1860 but the following year he resigned to become a colonel of the 86th Illinois Volunteers. He attained the rank of major general before the end of the Civil War.

Richard J. Oglesby was the only man elected Governor of the state of Illinois three times. He was so honored in 1864, 1872, and 1884. He did not serve the second term, however, as he was appointed United States Senator almost immediately after his inauguration. In 1889 he retired to his farm home, "Oglehurst," near Elkhart, Illinois, and he resided there until his death in 1899.

SACRAMENTO CITY, Aug. 12th, 1849.

Editors Illinois Journal:

Having arrived here in advance of the emigrant companies from Sangamon and the adjoining counties, I have thought it prudent to advise the friends of those who left that vicinity for California last spring, of their position, in the line of emigration. That many rumors of every cast, from moderate to extreme exaggeration, will reach the States, as to the fate of the emigrants, is more than probable. It then becomes a matter of importance to obtain as many truths as practicable, to allay the general excitement consequent upon such rumors; and having formed one of the emigration, and being to some extent familiar with suffering of the emigrants, these will briefly be related in plain style.

The Independent company, composed of Henry Sodoris, R. F. Piatt and George Matsler, of Piatt County—T. L. Loomis of Macoupin, N. W. Pedecord of Dewitt, and Henry Prather, Wm. Rea, Jacob Hummell and R. J. Oglesby of Macon county; with three wagons and 18 mules, left St. Joseph[1] on the 5th day of May, 1849. On the 6th day of May we passed in-camp Capt. Watson's mule train from Springfield, Ill. and Capt. Webber's[2] train from Sangamon county, all well, and ready to enter upon

---

[1] St. Joseph and Independence in Missouri, and Kanesville and Council Bluffs in Iowa were the chief points of departure for Forty-Niners intending to follow the Oregon or Mormon trails.

[2] B. A. Watson, John B. Watson, and J. B. Weber were members of the Illinois and California Mining Mutual Insurance Company. This group, twenty-one in number, left Springfield for California in March, 1849. *History of Sangamon County, Illinois*, published by the Inter-State Publishing Company (Chicago, 1881), 536.

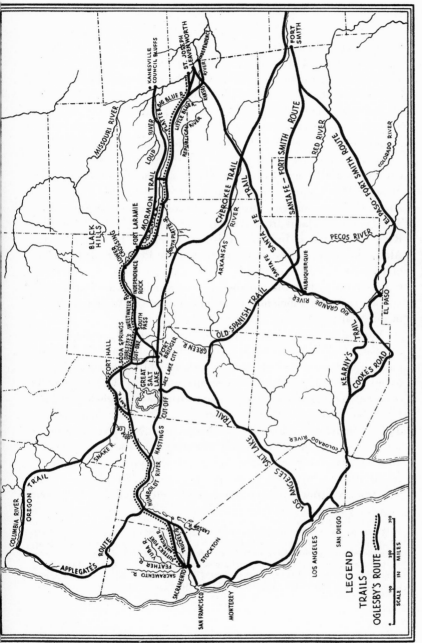

OVERLAND TRAILS, 1849

the journey. Three other wagons with ox teams, (Mr. Saunders one of them), lay at the upper ferry in readiness to start. No important circumstances or remarkable events beyond the ordinary difficulties attendant upon unpracticed emigrant parties, occurred for several days after our departure from St. Joseph. The trail was thickly studded with wagons, all moving on in comfortable order, at leisure. The Independent company reached Fort Larmime [Laramie][3] on the morning of the 5th June, 500 miles, according to daily computation, by the Road-ometer, passing in that distance 900 wagons, mostly ox teams. Up to this point grass abounded in sufficient supply to accommodate 10,000 teams. The extensive plains from the River of Wolves[4] to the little Blue River, were robed in the garniture of spring, fresh and green. Along the valley of the main channel of the Platte, and the vallies of the north and south forks of the same stream, the grass was rich and thick, but the narrow limit to which it was confined did not warrant its sufficiency to accommodate the numerous trains in our rear.

Various and conflicting statements had already preceded our company to Fort Laramie, as to the sufferings of the rear emigrant parties; but in every instance when thoroughly investigated, were found to be exaggerated and generally untrue.—The Independent company having made arrangements with the Springfield company to travel across the Plains in company with them, delayed one day for them at the Blue River to come up. Not having done so, we traveled to the South Fork of the Platte, and again delayed another day; but they did not come up. From the South Platte to the Ferry across the North Platte, distant 278 miles, the trail was thickly strewn with wagons, the teams of all of which were

---

[3] Fort Laramie was established by the American Fur Trading Company in 1834, but by 1849 it had been acquired by the United States government and was occupied by two companies of soldiers. Thick adobe walls, by this time in a dilapidated condition, enclosed the rectangular area of the post. Inside were a number of stores where emigrants could purchase supplies. Archer Butler Hulbert, *Forty-Niners, the Chronicle of the California Trail* (Boston, 1932), 110-11; Owen Cochran Coy, *The Great Trek* (Los Angeles, 1931), 139-40.

[4] Loup River.

in very fine order; no misfortunes having occurred to dampen or cast a shade of despondency over the vast and cheerful body. On this stream our company passed 200 trains, most of them in the Black Hills, or Stepping Stones to the Rocky Mountains; in this body were the Alton company, at Ash Hollow, the Macoupin county company from Woodburn, the Galena company and the Jersey county company; a large train. At this point the Independent company lay-by 3 days in waiting for the Springfield train. On the evening of the 3d day, having been ferried across the south fork of the Platte, we determined to continue on the trail, having been satisfactorily informed that the Springfield train was moving on in good order, and would not likely be up for another day.

From the ferry to Independence Rock,[5] on the Sweet Water River, a noted land mark, distant 60 miles, we found no grass and the water quite inferior,—strongly impregnated with Alkali and common Salt. On this stretch it is very fair to presume there will be slight suffering among the emigrants, moving by ox teams. From Independence Rock to the South Pass of the Rocky Mountains the general face of the country is broken and sterile, but grass and water at the time the Independent company passed this region, was found in sufficient quantities to accommodate the emigration in advance of us, and all we had up to this time passed. In the great South Pass and on to Green River via Sublett's cut-off—sometimes called Meek's cut-off—the indispensable requisite of grass and water to the welfare, in fact to the existence of emigrant parties, were found in such large abundance as to satisfy the demands of all the emigration from the United States for the present year, though it should exceed 100,000. But little sickness occurred among the emigration and no cases were known to have been fatal. Universal good health prevailed until after entering

---

[5] This rock reached a height of almost two hundred feet in some places and was about fifteen hundred yards in circumference. It was said to have been named by a party of trappers en route to Oregon who reached it on the Fourth of July, 1810 or 1811. One of its chief points of interest was a "Register," where the names of travelers who passed that way were carved in the rock. Many of these signatures were soon obliterated by the sandstorms which were prevalent in the region. Hulbert, *Forty-Niners*, 143-44.

the Rocky Mountains, when a few were attacked with the common disease of the region, known in common parlance as the Mountain Fever. On the 2d day of July our company reached Fort Hall—having up to this period passed all moving in fine style—1,300 wagons.

It is deemed useless to recount every change from the ordinary toils of a journey across the plains; to do so would be irksome and render this, otherwise brief narrative, a verbose and unreadable letter. We found the Fort in the occupation of the Hudson Bay Company, and somewhat dilapidated. It is at this point that emigrants to the Pacific ocean meet with a final opportunity of supplying themselves with such articles as are necessary to their comfort, and that, too, at exorbitant and unchristian prices. Men after long exposure and constant privation, unaccustomed to want for the necessaries of life, are fit subjects for speculation, upon reaching this distant and habited spot; and the avaricious occupants of the post lay hold upon them with the vigor of the leech, and cease not until the last farthing is exhausted. It is a matter of serious neglect that this important post, within the jurisdiction of the United States, should be permitted to remain in the possession of a foreign association, under the patronage of Great Britain, in a territory belonging exclusively to our own Government.[6] Large and astonishing profits are made by them in their trading with the numerous Indian tribes of that vicinity, and for that purpose those untutored children of the forest are kept in a vassalage of ignorance totally at variance with every christian principle—discreditable to the cause, and much to our

---

[6] Fort Hall was established in 1834 by Nathaniel J. Wyeth, a trader, who sold it to the Hudson's Bay Company in 1837. It was located on the Snake River, a fork of the Columbia River. According to the terms of the treaty this country made with Great Britain in 1846, the rights of the Hudson's Bay Company in the territory ceded to the United States were to be respected. At times supplies were so scarce at the fort that instead of selling to emigrants the company bought from some of them who happened to be overstocked and wished to lighten their burden. The post was abandoned about 1856. Hubert Howe Bancroft, *History of Oregon* (San Francisco, 1890), I: 14, II: 112; *Documents of American History*, edited by Henry Steel Commager (New York, 1934), 312; Hulbert, *Forty-Niners*, 175-76; Coy, *The Great Trek*, 156-59.

injury, as an enlightened people. During the few moments our
company remained at the Fort, I noticed three Shoshone Indians
offer for sale to the little white whiskered gentleman officiating
in the absence of Captain Grant,[7] as commandant, three Elk
skins, large and of a superior quality. In exchange they received
15 cts each in powder, one flint and 15 bullets. I also noticed the
same skins offered to emigrants at $5.00 each, in less than five
minutes.

From Fort Hall the trail, after driving north to the 43d parallel,
again assumes a south west course, leading over the great dividing
Ridge, 230 miles to the head of Humbolt River,[8] down into the
interior Basin of California, leaving the Oregon route at Raft
River, 60 miles south west of Fort Hall. This is a hard portion
of the route to travel over; grass exists in very limited quantities,
scattered sparely along the margin of small mountain streams,
dry but quite nutricious. It was lamentable to find that the few
teams yet in advance, had nearly exhausted the supply, except
on goose river. If the rear trains will be able to reach this river—
and doubtless they will, grass will be found in abundance of the
most nutricious quality, including the valuable Mountain bunch
grass, and Buffalo grass, either of which afford an ample substitute
for corn or oats; and here they can recruit their jaded stock, and
prepare for the desert before them.

In fact from St. Joseph, on to this river, or even down to Humbolt, alias Mary's Sink River, there is no obstacle which can really
be conceived as insurmountable by the emigrants. That there
will be exposure and some privation both to man and beast, is not
to be questioned. It was in the out-set expected, and generally
prepared against, at least by a stout resolution to overcome it,
and they will succeed. As we passed over this region of country—
quite indeed unfit for the habitation of civilized men—we saw
nothing of the living kind roaming over it save a few straggling
digger Indians and Scorpions. The reflection involuntarily arose,

---

[7] James Grant. Bancroft, *History of Oregon*, I: 42n.
[8] Humboldt River.

what will be the fate of the rear emigrants; but the constant reports brought forward by the pack mule trains, gave every assurance that there was not the slightest hardship among them.

After reaching the north fork of Mary's Sink river, recently named in *honor* of the "Nestor of scientific travelers" called Humbolt river (though myself, I think, a disparagement to the fame of that distinguished gentleman), we had but a few messages from the rear parties.—If any where, however, betwixt this city and St. Joseph, the emigrants are expected to suffer, it will be upon this miserable stream, puffed and blown up by the scientific travelers, who have undertaken to give a faithful Geographical description of California; we were well prepared to be seriously, in fact injuriously disappointed, in this water course and its vallies. By many of the emigrants it had been regarded as a Italian Paradise, and earnestly and laboriously sought as an oasis in a desert—a home in a wilderness, where the weary emigrant, worn down by the toils of a long and lonesome journey, might recline upon its soft field of rich green grass, and repose in ease among its pastoral lawns and shady bowers—but, alas! foul illusion! how bitter the remembrance! When the promised goal was obtained; and the glad hearted emigrant supposed himself in the midst of a bountiful harvest, the reality exhibited itself, and Mary's Sink River was seen to be a barren desolate stream, meandering betwixt two sandy banks, affording life to a few dejected willows, too low to offer even a shade to the semi-cannibals alone inhabiting its repulsive shores. The vallies of the stream are narrow, composed chiefly of sand, salaratus, common salt and sulphur, giving no sustenance to any species of vegetation whatever. It is 275 miles from the point at which the trail strikes it to the Sink; or that portion of it where the soil upon which it runs is too weak from want of strength to hold it up; the water does not sink, but becomes so sluggish that it ceases to flow and is taken up by the intense heat of the sun shining with unobstructed brilliancy all day. There is not enough grass, from the union of the forks of Mary's river to its Sink, to accommodate ten yoke of oxen one month—and the small quantity we found was so dry and salty that the mules refused to eat it, until absolute hunger drove them to it. The grass seemed to create a fever in the animals after eating it, and they would drink to such an excess as to arouse alarms for their safety.

We were overtaken by Captain Bryant,[9] the author of "What I saw in California," near the Sink, and he expressed much astonishment in finding the valley of the river so destitute of vegetation. From the Sink to Carson's river, distant 45 miles,—the same distance to Salmon Trout river[10]—there is a sand desert. This stretch finally terminates the only remaining doubtful impediments to the successful journey of the emigrants across the plains to the Sacramento river.

It may be that large numbers of the rear train will drive down to the Salt Lake city, and remain there until next spring. We have already reports that many of them have taken the Oregon route. Perhaps if these two expedients are adopted, the residue, by great caution and some suffering, will reach Carson river,— when they will be secure the residue of the trip, as it affords an abundance of rich grass, until the trail leaves at Pass Creek Cannon, to cross the Sierra Nevada.

At the time the "Independent Company" crossed the sand desert, lying between the Sink and Carson river, there were many evidences of suffering by those who had preceded us. The mouldering bodies and bleached bones, strewed along the trail, were ghastly witnesses of the destruction among the animals of the foremost trains. Oxen and mules, when they reach the desert, become so weak from want of food in coming down the river, that it requires two days or more to pass over the desert. In this time, laboring under a burning sun, they are so thirsty that many of them fall dead in their tracks, and leave the emigrants

    [9] Edwin Bryant. The first edition of this book was published in 1848.

    [10] Truckee River. John C. Fremont called it the Salmon Trout River because of the abundance of these fish he found there when he discovered it in 1844. J. C. Fremont, *Report of the Exploring Expedition to the Rocky Mountains* (Washington, 1845), 219; Joseph E. Ware, *The Emigrants' Guide to California*, reprinted from the 1849 edition with introduction and notes by John Caughey (Princeton, 1932), 36.

to walk the rest of the way for water, to save their own lives. Wells have been dug along near the trail, which afford large quantities of water; but it is too salt for use. Shortly after crossing this sterile tract, we had reports of several deaths on the desert from thirst; but these reports could scarcely be relied on.

On the morning the company left its camp, near the border of the desert, a married lady came in on horseback, bringing several canteens for water. She had left her husband and only child, late the evening before, some fifteen miles back, suffering for water, and in her anxiety to hasten to the river, had lost the trail and traveled the whole night;—but with that love which a mother only commands for a helpless and suffering, aye, dying child, she refused assistance, and would not weary until the holy mission was fulfilled. She delayed but a moment until the vessels were filled, when, being provided with a fresh horse, she flew with the speed of the arrow back to her suffering companion and dying child. This was an instance of personal devotion, and female heroism, I had never seen equalled.

Early on the morning of the 10th of August, safely and in good health, we encamped at Suter's Fort,[11] through in 95 days, 20 of which we did not travel,—preceded by 109 wagons,—having passed 1600 on the trail. Our mules were in nearly as good order the day we arrived here, as on the 5th of May,—having traveled, according to each day's estimate by the roadometer, 1960 miles from St. Joseph, via Forts Laramie and Hall, to the Sacramento river.

We are at present encamped near Sacramento city, a large place, recently built at the Embarcadora,[12] but now numbering

[11] Captain John A. Sutter obtained a grant of land from the Mexican government in 1840. He built a fort on a branch of the American River which became the center of the fur-trading and agricultural activities of his colony. With the discovery of gold in 1848, these enterprises lost their importance but Sutter soon adapted his post to the new requirements. His residence was converted into a hotel, and a taproom, billiard hall and hospital were installed in some of the other buildings. Dan Elbert Clark, *The West in American History* (New York, 1937), 479-80; Fremont, *Report of Expedition*, 246; Hulbert, *Forty-Niners*, 297-98.

[12] Embarcadero is the Spanish word for wharf or quay. Sacramento, founded in 1848, was located on the left bank of the Sacramento River.

5,000 souls, and rapidly increasing. From 10 to 20 houses go up in a day; but in consequence of the scarcity of lumber, and no other available substitute being at hand, factory cotton is chiefly used in the construction of buildings; which circumstance has obtained for the city the cognomen of "Ragtown."[13] During the short time we have been here, but few emigrant wagons have come in. Many of the emigrants will be likely to remain in the mines at various diggings,—as all articles of consumption by the miners are readily furnished at those points, by merchants at the towns along the Sacramento, the Yuba and Feather river, and the north and south forks of the American river. The San Cosummes and Callama[14] diggins are from 25 miles to 75 miles distant from this city.

Daily accounts are received from all those Diggins of large fortunes being acquired in a few days. I have seen several of the emigrants who came over this year, depositing with the merchants of this city, each from $500 to $5,000, obtained from the mines since arriving here. The gold occurs in spangles, mostly, however, in gold dust, but frequently in pepitas;—the auriferous deposits are chiefly among the large rocks in the bed of the channel of the river, and is disseminated similar to the deposits represented in the Ural districts of Russian Siberia. The depth of the deposits have not been accurately discovered, but range from one to fifteen feet. The washers in use are the common rocker and pan, and from one to three ounces avordupoise is considered a day's work, laboring five hours with either of these instruments. The rocker is so constructed that either one, or any other number of men, up to six may work them. The dust when obtained is usually carried in large buck-skin purses or bags, to the different towns convenient to the mines, and deposited for safe keeping at the rate of one per cent. per month, whilst the regulated interest upon

---

[13] This name must have been freely applied to hastily built towns. One such settlement, on the Carson River, was said to have been named from the "interminable piles of wind-strewn rags discarded by the emigration." Hulbert, *Forty-Niners*, 243, 252, 256.

[14] Coloma.

coin loaned in California near the mines is 10 per cent. per month.

As regards the state of society in those parts of California over which I have traveled, especially in the mines and towns near them, it is all as moral as could be desired, and far surpasses the expectations of every one—no murdering, no riots, and but little drunkenness—far less of this latter evil than is seen in the country towns of Illinois. A strict compliance with contracts, and a universal desire to preserve order and good feeling among the citizens, seems to be the ambition of every man. There is no law save that of nature, and the promptings of a good conscience; nor need there be so long as the present state of society exists—until California can have a regular government given her by the proper authority. Some pretension is made to enforce the old laws of the country prevailing previous to the acquisition of the Territory by the United States; but the measure is not popular—the Alcalde[15] is found to possess too much power to be exercised at discretion—from which there is no appeal.

We are now in the midst of the dry season, which I am informed is considered the sickly season of the year, and yet few persons are unwell. Doct. Zabriskie, who was from Jacksonville, Ills., a prominent physician of this city, assures me that the same amount of disease prevailing now might occur at any time during the year.

The following prices of articles are permanent in this city:— Mules, ordinary, $150; good mules $200 to $250; wagons for four and six mules or oxen $400 to $700; bacon 50 cts. per lb.; mess pork $50 per bbl.; mowing scythes $50 a piece; flour $16 per bbl.; fresh beef 50 cts. per lb.; butter $1 per lb.; lard 50 cts. per lb.; cheese $1 per lb.; whiskey $2.50 per quart; brandy $4; gin $1.50; and everything else in proportion, save Physicians' bills —they are from $10 to one ounce of gold for a single visit on foot about the city.

Concerning the exciting reports circulated through the United States previous to the 5th of May, 1849, in the public journals,

---

[15] Alcalde is the Spanish term for mayor of a town. He exercises certain judicial powers in addition to his regular duties.

in relation to the large amounts of gold obtained by individuals in the mines, from what I have seen might be regarded as generally true. Such accounts, for years to come, must be received from this El dorado, which as yet has scarcely been scratched.

Respectfully yours,

RICH'D J. OGLESBY.

OFFICIAL PROCEEDINGS
1938

REPORT OF THE SECRETARY

To the Directors of the Illinois State Historical Society:

GENTLEMEN:

I present herewith a summary of the activities of the Illinois State Historical Society since the last annual meeting, May 14, 1937.

The Society held its usual Illinois Day meeting in Springfield on December 3, 1937. Because of the illness of President James, Mr. Frank E. Stevens, one of the Society's Vice-Presidents, presided. The address of the occasion was delivered by Mr. Douglas C. McMurtrie, noted typographer and authority on the history of printing, who spoke on the subject, "The Contribution of the Pioneer Printers to Illinois History." After the address, a reception was held in the Illinois State Historical Library, where examples of the work of the printers whom Mr. McMurtrie had discussed were on display.

In my report of a year ago I announced that fifty-three new members had been admitted to membership in the year 1936-37, and that for the first time in several years the Society's membership showed a net increase. I now take pleasure in reporting that since May 14, 1937, 212 new members have joined the Society. This represents by far the largest increase in our membership for many years. The net gain, however, has been smaller than these figures would indicate. The practice of the past has been to retain members of our active list even though no dues had been paid for several years. Now members are billed in advance at the beginning of each calendar year. If dues remain unpaid for that year, and the year which follows, a final notice is sent. If this is disregarded, the membership is cancelled.

The membership gain which I have noted is in part the result of systematic effort by the officers of the Society; but it is also the result of the increased attractiveness of the Society's *Journal*.

You may recall that a year ago I recommended certain changes in both the format and content of this publication. Your President appointed a committee to act upon that recommendation. The *Journal* as it now appears is that committee's work. The publication of the first number in the new format occasioned much favorable comment from members, from the press, and from officials of other historical societies. Several competent judges have expressed the opinion that the *Journal* of the Illinois State Historical Society is now equalled by few similar publications and surpassed by none.

In my opinion, the Society's annual volume of *Transactions* needs redesigning even more than the *Journal* before its rejuvenation. In both title and format, the *Transactions* is forbidding, and no poorer arrangement than the present practice of putting minutes and reports at the beginning of the volume could possibly be devised. I recommend, therefore, that the title of this book be changed to *Papers in Illinois History*, that it be redesigned throughout and that the reports of official proceedings be relegated to the back of the book where they will not discourage the reader whose interest is in the subject matter of history.

During the year just past the Secretary of the Society has been called upon to participate in historical activities of many kinds. He has filled numerous speaking engagements, and in general co-operated fully in all projects within the scope of the Society's interests. One of these deserves mention in some detail.

In the heart of Springfield, in daily use as the courthouse of Sangamon County, stands the structure which served as the state house of Illinois from 1837 until 1875. No building in Illinois has richer associations with the great figures of Illinois history, and particularly with the life of Abraham Lincoln. Aware of this fact, many people of the state have long felt that the use of the building by Sangamon County should be discontinued, and that it should be made a permanent memorial to Abraham Lincoln. Practical difficulties, mainly financial, have long prevented the realization of this hope.

Recently, however, there appeared to be a possibility of achieving the desired result through a combination of WPA projects looking toward the construction of a new city-county building for Springfield. This plan depended in part upon the purchase of the old State House by the State of Illinois. The purchase was considered impracticable by the state authorities— partly because insufficient time for securing the necessary appropriations was available; partly because of the lack of a carefully considered plan for the building's utilization. As a result, the entire matter was dropped.

The discussions, however, served to emphasize the necessity of a detailed plan for the use of the Old State House should it ever be made a memorial. There was general agreement, moreover, that the proper organization to formulate such a plan was the Illinois State Historical Society. If the Society itself is willing to assume this responsibility, it will be faced with a task of some difficulty. Museum treatment is indicated, but the museum technique is a highly specialized one with which no member of the Society's staff is familiar. It should be possible to secure technical assistance—possibly from the National Park Service— but such assistance might require a considerable expenditure. I believe the project to be a proper one for the Society to undertake if the expense in connection with it can be limited to a reasonable figure.

During the past year three Directors of the Society have died —Laurence M. Larson of Urbana, Cornelius J. Doyle of Springfield, and Henry J. Patten of Evanston. The Society will undoubtedly wish to memorialize the long and loyal services of these men in an appropriate manner.

In the Society's general membership, the following deaths have occurred since the last annual meeting:

Mrs. Frank J. Bowman............................Sterling
Harry S. Calver................................Elyria, Ohio
Fred E. Carpenter................................Rockford
W. H. Conway....................................Springfield

C. P. Dadant.....................................Hamilton
E. F. Dunne.......................................Chicago
Rev. C. J. Eschmann.............................Waterloo
Dr. Elmer E. Hagler............................Springfield
Richard Yates Hoffman...........................Chicago
Mrs. Henry Needles.........................Granite City
Vincent J. Root....................................Galva
Mrs. Martin Ryerson.............................Chicago
W. B. Strang...................................Roodhouse
Frank L. Trutter..............................Springfield

Respectfully submitted,

PAUL M. ANGLE.

ANNUAL BUSINESS MEETING
ILLINOIS STATE HISTORICAL SOCIETY
NORMAL, ILLINOIS, MAY 14, 1938

President James called the meeting to order. A quorum being present, Mr. Angle presented his reports as Secretary-Treasurer, which were accepted and approved. Various matters covered in these reports were then discussed and disposed of as follows:

The following resolution relating to the Old State House in Springfield was passed unanimously:

WHEREAS, The Old State House in Springfield (now owned and occupied as a courthouse by the County of Sangamon) served as the Capitol of Illinois for nearly forty years, and

WHEREAS, The Old State House in its original form was a building of distinguished architectural design, and

WHEREAS, The lives of many of the most distinguished citizens of this state—notably Abraham Lincoln, Stephen A. Douglas, U. S. Grant, and Richard Yates—were intimately associated with this structure:

Be it resolved by the Illinois State Historical Society that the acquisition of the Old State House by the State of Illinois, its restoration to its original appearance, and its preservation as an historical museum constitute an end greatly to be desired, and one which deserves the support of all persons interested in the history of this State.

Mr. Angle stated that the acquisition of the Old State House might depend in large part upon the formulation of a suitable plan for its use, and asserted that he knew that any plan for the use of the structure which might be formulated by the Illinois State Historical Society would be welcomed by those who were interested in the project. Therefore it was moved, seconded and passed that President James be requested to appoint a committee to devise such a plan. Mr. Angle stated that he had already requested the National Park Service to make a museum technician available to the Society for this purpose.

Mr. Angle stated that a movement was on foot at Galena to erect there an historical museum (to be known as the Hall of Fame) and that he had been asked to find out whether the Society would consider making a financial contribution to the project. After discussion it was moved, seconded and passed that the proposal to create an historical museum at Galena be endorsed and aided in all ways not requiring the expenditure of funds on the part of the Society.

Mr. Angle then brought up for consideration the question of the continuance of the Society's subvention towards the cost of the publication, *Writings in American History*. The opinion prevailed that the value of this publication was greatly impaired by the growing interval between the year it covers and the date of its appearance. However, a subvention of $50 for one year was voted, but the Secretary was instructed to notify those in charge of the publication that the contribution would probably not be continued unless steps were taken to bring it out more nearly on time.

The question of awarding a medal for distinguished work in Illinois history was then brought up for discussion. Various objections were mentioned—principally the cost of the dies for a medal, and the tendency of awards to become the subject of intrigue on the part of self-appointed recipients. Those present, however, expressed themselves in favor of some kind of an award to be bestowed by the Society. President James was requested to appoint a committee to consider the question and make a definite recommendation to the Society at its next annual meeting.

President James expressed, on behalf of its members, the Society's appreciation of the effective co-operation of the McLean County Historical Society. It was that co-operation, he said, which had made the Bloomington-Normal meeting one of the most successful in the Society's history. The meeting was proof of the interest in the history of the State, and indicated the possibilities for enlargement and increased effectiveness which faced the Society. One immediate objective should be the addition of 500 members before the next annual meeting—a goal which could easily be attained if the Directors would devote time and effort to it.

President James reminded the members of the Society that because of illness, Professor Pease was absent for the first time in many years.   Whereupon the following resolution was passed unanimously:

> The members of the Illinois State Historical Society learn with regret that illness has prevented one of our Vice-Presidents and Directors, Theodore C. Pease, from attending this annual meeting.   We resolve, therefore, that the Secretary be requested to convey to Professor Pease our sympathy and our hope for his speedy and complete recovery.

President James then notified the Society of the recent death of Marcus L. Hansen, Professor of History at the University of Illinois and well-known historian.   Whereupon the following resolution was adopted:

> The members of the Illinois State Historical Society have learned of the death of Marcus Lee Hansen with profound regret.   His achievements in the field of history were substantial, and we who knew him looked upon what he had done as the certain promise of greater contributions in the future. His death deprives American historical scholarship of one of its most brilliant expositors, and deprives us of a fellow-member and friend.
>
> *Be it resolved*, therefore, that we give formal expression to our sorrow at the passing of Marcus Lee Hansen, and that we convey to the surviving members of his family our heartfelt sympathy.

President James informed the Society that three of its Directors had died since the last annual meeting—Laurence M. Larson, Cornelius J. Doyle, and Henry J. Patten.   The Society then adopted the following resolutions:

> The death of Laurence M. Larson has deprived the world of scholarship of one of its greatest figures—a man who had earned the high honor which his colleagues had bestowed

upon him by his solid achievements in research, his extraordinary skill as a teacher, his effective administration of a department in a great university, and his kindly and ever-helpful personality. To have enjoyed the services, as a member of the Board of Directors, of such a man has been an honor of which the members of this Society will ever be mindful; to have this association of many years' duration severed is the cause of profound regret and sorrow.

Be it Resolved, Therefore, that we, the members of the Illinois State Historical Society give expression to our grief at the passing of Laurence M. Larson, and that we have our heartfelt sympathy conveyed to the surviving members of his family.

Whereas, The death of Cornelius J. Doyle has occurred since the last meeting of this Society, and

Whereas, Mr. Doyle was for many years a Director of this Society, and an active participant, both as a public official and as a private citizen, in all movements for the preservation and dissemination of the history of Illinois,

Be it Resolved, That the Illinois State Historical Society take this means of acknowledging the loss it has suffered by his death, and

Be it Further Resolved, That these resolutions be spread upon the records of the Society, printed in its publication, and transmitted, with the sympathy of this membership, to the surviving members of his family.

Whereas, the death of Henry J. Patten has occurred since the last annual meeting of this Society, and

Whereas, Mr. Patten was for many years a Director of this Society, a faithful attendant at its meetings, and an effective worker for the accomplishment of its purposes,

Be it Resolved, That the Illinois State Historical Society take this means of acknowledging the loss it has suffered by his death, and

Be it Further Resolved, That these resolutions be spread upon the records of the Society, printed in its publication, and transmitted, with the sympathy of this membership, to the surviving members of his family.

At the suggestion of the Secretary the advisability of holding the Society's annual meetings in early October rather than in May was discussed, but no conclusion was reached.

President James stated that the Society had received invitations to hold its next annual meeting in Quincy and Carbondale. Upon the recommendation of the Board of Directors the Quincy invitation, tendered by the Quincy Historical Society, was accepted. The Secretary was requested to advise the officials of the Southern Illinois State Normal University that an invitation to hold the 1940 meeting at Carbondale would be received with favor.

The session devoted to the teaching of Illinois history having aroused much interest and a generally favorable reaction, it was the opinion of the meeting that President James should appoint a committee representing the Society to wait upon the state course of study committee headed by Professor S. E. Thomas and urge that provision for the teaching of Illinois history be made.

By unanimous vote, Arthur Andersen[1] of Chicago and James G. Randall of Urbana were elected to the Board of Directors to fill the unexpired terms of Laurence M. Larson and Cornelius J. Doyle.

By unanimous vote, Ernest E. East, Peoria; Logan Hay, Springfield; Wayne C. Townley, Bloomington; Jewell F. Stevens, Chicago; and Oliver R. Barrett, Chicago; were elected to the Board of Directors for terms of three years each.

The meeting then adjourned.

MEETING OF THE BOARD OF DIRECTORS
ILLINOIS STATE HISTORICAL SOCIETY
NORMAL, ILLINOIS, MAY 14, 1938

Present: James A. James, Mrs. Henry English, Ernest E. East, Jewell F. Stevens, Wayne C. Townley, Clint Clay Tilton, Paul M. Angle, James G. Randall.

By unanimous vote, the following officers were elected: President, James A. James; First Vice-President, Clint Clay Tilton; Vice-Presidents, Theodore C. Pease, Evarts Boutell Greene, John H. Hauberg, George W. Smith, Frank E. Stevens; Secretary-Treasurer, Paul M. Angle.

The report of the Secretary-Treasurer was accepted and approved.

By unanimous vote, the salary of the Secretary-Treasurer was increased from $500 annually to $750 per year, payable semi-annually.

The following budget for the ensuing year was adopted:

Historical Markers........................$300
Expense of meetings...................... 300
Temporary assistants..................... 300
Salary Secretary-Treasurer............... 750
Miscellaneous expenses................... 500

By vote of the Directors the President was requested to appoint an auditing committee whose duty it should be to examine the books of the Society and report to the Directors at the time of the next annual meeting.

The meeting then adjourned.

THE ILLINOIS STATE HISTORICAL SOCIETY

OFFICERS, 1938-1939

INDEX